MW01611332

Dance Your Way to Spirit
with Adnan Sarhan

*Adnan's Students Relate Their
Remarkable and Joyful Experiences
on the Way to Spirit*

**Sufi Foundation of America
Torreon, NM**

Published by:
Sufi Foundation of America
P.O. Box 170
Torreon, NM 87061
(505)384-5135

Edited by Gwen Gosé and Dr. Michelle Peticolas

Cover art by Adnan Sarhan

ISBN: 1-884328-10-5

Printed and bound in the United States of America

Printed on acid-free papers

"The dance is the yearning of the spirit to free-dom."

"The dance becomes the life of the moment. When you are in the moment, the moment expands and becomes a tranquil sea of time."

"To go to the spirit, you will get the spirit."
-- Adnan Sarhan

About Adnan Sarhan . . .

Sufi Master Adnan Sarhan is director of the Sufi Foundation of America and a member of five Sufi orders: Qadri, Naqshibandi, Rafai, Mevlevi, and Malamati. Internationally known for the Shattari (Rapid) Method, his work develops higher intelligence and awareness, and causes people to become creative and innovative by destroying all types of bad habits.

Adnan leads participants in a wide range of timeless techniques. Based on various traditions of scholarship, meditative sciences, physical exercise, mystical dance and music, the work signals a connection to the past which stretches back twelve hundred years. Exercises, meditation, drumming, movement, dancing and whirling are used to develop the higher intelligence of the heart, improve will power, heighten concentration, bring better personality, produce bodily changes like slower heart rates and lower blood pressure, and produce shifts in perception which result in clarity of thinking, improved memory and positive attitude.

Over the years, Adnan has conducted workshops at prestigious institutions throughout the United States and many other countries of the world including the United Nations in New York, St. James' Church in London, Alhambra Palace in Granada, Spain, the World Congress of Psychology in Switzerland, a grand concert at the Otto Zutz in Barcelona, Spain, the Earth Summit in Brazil, the Cathedral Church of St. John the Divine, New York, the Unitarian Society of Whittier, California, Esalen Institute in Big Sur, California, and conferences of Humanistic Psychology.

Last year he received a special invitation from the Russian Parliament to visit Moscow. Each summer he directs an intensive two month workshop at the Sufi Foundation Retreat Center in the Manzano Mountains of New Mexico. For further information about the summer program and Adnan's touring schedule, contact:

Sufi Foundation of America
P.O. Box 170
Torreon, NM 87061
(505) 384-5135

Contents

Preface

Dr. Michelle Peticolas and Gwen Gosé, Poet-In-Residence

Sometimes during the final weeks of camp, Adnan's students write about their various experiences of the summer. The following are a selection of reports written over the past decade which reveal a remarkable change in quality and content from earlier times. Not only are they written with creativity, imagination and style, but they also indicate a deep and profound understanding of the Sufi work with Adnan and a comprehension of its impact on people's lives.

Adnan has suggested to "write about how the work has affected your habits and conditioning." One would expect the usual score of remarkable testimonials of quitting smoking, drinking, drugs, over-eating, etc., as the work is very effective in eliminating these habits. But many of the reports go beyond the obvious physical addictions to examine a more subtle and insidious set of conditioned behavioral patterns, like attachments to pride, criticism, jealousy, success, intellect, identity and ego. These discussions show a remarkable insight into the very process of spiritual change and development, and imply that purification of the body from chemical addictions and bad eating habits is but one of the first steps. Ridding the mind of distracting behavioral patterns and emotional blocks runs in second. The glorious conclusion that could be drawn suggests that when these weights and chains are shed, the heart becomes light and free. It soars like the birds and plays among the clouds, and the universe expands to unfold in all its brilliance and the moment opens in pure ecstasy.

"Nothing benefits the heart more than a spiritual retreat wherein it enters the domain of meditation." -- Ibn 'Ata'illah

Light, Life and Love
Marjana Tracy

After many years of searching and yearning, I was guided to Adnan. Initially, I took a long look at the teacher, I questioned the students, I doubted myself and my capacity, but I do not ever remember doubting the work. It was the first time in my life that I did not doubt. I have been in the work four years now. At times I have been distracted, inattentive, confused, resentful, and exhausted, but I have never left the work because it has not left me.

When I have burned parts of my self in self-created hells, the work has flowed over me time and time again to quench the flames. Sometimes the fires last a very long time and just as I fear they are blazing out of control, I am blessed with the cool waters of the work. The blessings seem further apart now than in the beginning. I was showered with blessings early in the work as if it would prove to me that there was much to look forward to. Then the blessings made less frequent appearances as though to remind me that blessings are earned and a disciple must have discipline. Now, when they come, each one is more precious than the last. The years elapse as I creep along the path toward the unknown.

This summer I have understood why I avoided psychologists and psychics, and why I instinctively trusted Adnan's work. Psychologists and psychics are in the business of helping people answer the who am I question. Adnan's words ring through my ears, "*Men anna, anna hunna.* Who am I? I exist. To exist is a miracle, to live is an opportunity." For me, that is enough. It is not enough for people who relate to reality through the intellect alone. The intellect is insatiable and the mind will create more questions and answers than the life can hold. The whole life could be spent doing nothing but answering theoretical questions with rational concepts. ˙

I am no longer interested in who I am. I do not feel a need to define the "I" or the ego by connecting it to past conditioning, emotions, ideas, thoughts and opinions. It is a tiresome process. In Adnan's work it is possible to see all those things in the blink of an eye and to go beyond them. Instead of digging in dark rocky caves of the self, it is possible to simply see what is in the cave and move on up into the light. Why pick at the carcass of the self when the spirit, which contains the universe, waits to be explored?

Back to the light. Adnan often hypnotizes us with repetitive ensnaring prose. "The love is light and the light is love. And the love is love and the love is life. And the life is love . And God guides the worthy ones to the light." I have read these words from his book so many times and have always been profoundly effected by them. Effected but not affected: touched but not changed. I cried but did not know why. This summer I know why. I have made my own connections between light and life and love. Until people do this for themselves words remain only words. After words are experienced they become reality. This is why the lips of wisdom are sealed but to the ears of understanding. Or as Adnan says, "The secret protects itself." This new understanding has given me an enormous sense of freedom and peace.

"Respect the time and your spirit becomes a child, and the time is its playmate, like two beautiful children rolling on the beach between the waves and the sun." – Adnan

Odile Discovers Her World as Food
Odile Atthalin

At the end of the first session of Adnan's workshop in Paris, I found myself in an exalted state of high energy and fulfillment. This work was IT! The most perfected form of any body work I had come across in my years of search, and I was seized by a voracious appetite to devour it in a whole new frenzy of wanting, grabbing, acquiring -- Adnan's energy, techniques, skills, science of timing, all the qualities that make up the beauty of his work. In that state, I came to this summer workshop, in order to become another Adnan as fast as possible. And I was convinced that after two months, 24 hours-a-day of that, I would have it all down. I would have eaten up the juice, the pulp, and the skin, and would own a whole new set of possessions, tools, gadgets for my personal gratification and professional profit. After the first few days, it seemed I was going to be fed exactly the food I expected. But soon, the long moments of rest, before, in the middle, or at the end of the exercises, became more important--moments of meditation I had never known before, not that slow drowning into a pool of muddy waters, but a delicious stillness. The work was touching another level, not only the physical body and its greed for attention, but bringing an awareness of old tension and let-go.

At this point, the idea of fasting was in the air and I thought I would try it and add one more experience to my collection. At the same time a book was read to the group from which I heard three words that struck a chord, even a gong inside, and awakened something. The words were "world as food." It seemed to describe my general attitude toward the world, a compulsion to have, absorb, devour, swallow all the experiences it can offer-- sensual, emotional, intellectual, and also, spiritual. And that it was what I was doing here with this workshop--stuffing myself more and more and more, and creating that tension of never having enough. And the question arising: "What am I doing all this for?" The fast came in time to break this pattern by separating me from food. It seemed to separate me from the attitude of constant wanting and having and gave me a sense of freedom totally new. I remember the feeling of release one of the first days of the fast when I could walk by a bunch of enticing red berries without having to grab them, but allowing them to have their own destiny. And also I had the feeling that I was being fed in a natural way by the air I was breathing, by the vibrations of the trees and of the wind, by the energy source, by Adnan, by the support of the group, by the eyes, the smiles, the moves, the dance, the love of all the environment. New waves of let-go and unconscious tensions melted away. And, one day after whirling, laying down in the grass, I had the feeling the earth was breathing with me or me with the earth and all around, an expansion that only this subtle kind of food could give. And my attitude was shifting from "wanting- having" to "being with" and a feeling of fluidity, felt as compassion, opened to the all-pervading love.

Then I could see that behind all the tools Adnan works with, a deeper substance is experienced by the people, a rich vibrant substance that could be called "peace". It's another level of relaxation, and from that state of peace and involvement in the moment sprouts different forms and shapes of dance, just as a seed sprouts to become a tree.

It is true, coming out of the world of food through fasting is like being born out of the womb of infancy into a world of abundance, a garden of delights, where God provides.

Today, I feel like a maple leaf, swaying and dancing in the breeze with millions of other maple leaves, transforming sun energy into the chlorophyll green of peace.

Thank you to Adnan, the Alchemical Master of the Feast.

"The spirit is a fountain of a lake of tranquil thought, and peace is its echo." – Adnan

Rachel's Peace and Miracle
Rachel Kaplan

For the first time in my life I have chosen to be peaceful and grateful. I am growing to understand how to protect the peace and gratitude from onslaughts of anger, self-doubt and melancholy. I have been chanting nearly daily this year. I began, I will admit, because Adnan said during the Christmas workshop, "Chant every day and you will get a miracle." It is just tonight in writing this that I discover I have received a miracle.

"All remembrance (chanting) defies all thoughts of the world." – Jaifar

The Awakening of Rambha
Rambha Niembro

I am an airline hostess for Iberian Airlines, a Spanish company. I have worked as a "stew" for 14 years, travelling all over the world. I also have being doing spiritual work for 14 years.

I started in 1969 with Majarishi Mahesh Yogi's Transcendental Meditation. I spent one year with him in the south of Spain, training to become a teacher of his technique. Later, with some other people of that movement, I started the first TM center in Madrid. I worked there at the center part-time, when I wasn't flying. While I practiced and taught TM, I was at the same time looking into other spiritual disciplines available in India and Europe and had contact with the paths of Guru Mahariashi, Guru Raj, Sivananda, Hare Krishna and several others.

In 1976, I met Swami Muktananda in Paris and I was so impressed with him and his meditation that I went to his ashram in India. After my stay in India, I returned to Spain and opened the first Madrid Muktananda Center in my house. There I began teaching Siddha Yoga. It was the beginning of four years for me as a Siddha devotee. By that time, I was vegetarian and a non-smoker and I used to get up every morning at three or four a.m. to meditate and chant, even when I was on my regular flying schedule!

It was in 1978 or early 1979 that I met Adnan. He was on his first visit to Spain and came one evening to the house to have dinner with us. I remember that on that occasion he suggested that I do Sufi work. But at that time I was too fanatic and proud of what I was doing, thinking that what I was doing was the "best" and I didn't want to get into anything else, let alone Sufi work.

Soon after this meeting with Adnan something changed for me and I started to go from one extreme to the other. I started to meditate less frequently and began going out to discos and associating with some of the crazier people of Madrid. I also became the worst drug addict you ever saw. For the next three years I was taking heroine and cocaine every single day. I don't know why I went from one extreme to the other, but whatever it was, it seemed to have had something to do with not being balanced. With Siddha ritual, I was too much on the intellectual level, thinking I possessed the "truth" and this was not practical at all, as Adnan was to later explain when I met him again in Spain, on the island of Mallorca in May of 1982.

At the time of this second meeting, I was in a terrible state, let me tell you. Shortly before, I had been released from prison and had moved from Madrid to Mallorca with the intention of changing my life, my circle of friends and giving up my addictions. But you can't run away from yourself. Naturally, that was precisely what happened to me. I continued taking heroine and cocaine regularly, right up until the day Adnan reentered my life. I remember Adnan's words when he saw me. "You look better than ever," he said. He had recognized me and had remembered who I was and his compliment was a boost of optimism and hope. For the first time in three years, I felt that perhaps the drug addiction problem I had could be done away with.

In those four years that passed between my first meeting with Adnan and my rediscovery of him, I had tried everything: detoxification programs in Spain and the United States, more meditation systems, doctors, psychiatrists, but nothing worked. Not even being in prison made me drop the drug habit. I could only pray to God to get me out of the mess I was in because I knew I couldn't deal with any of it any longer. I was down and out. A heroine addict is the saddest of sad things. You stop being a human being. A dog is much better off.

In Mallorca that first day, Adnan said to me, "Come for this weekend's workshop and your life will change." I can't say why but I trusted him completely. Something told me to try it, even in the face of my previous failures. And I couldn't possibly lose anything by it. The idea stayed with me and Adnan's personality attracted me much more than the first time I met him. Anyway, I got into the Sufi work on that first weekend.

When I went home after that workshop, everyone in the house where I was living was stoned on drugs. My "friends" insisted that I take some drugs, too. But something very strong said I didn't want it anymore. Since then I haven't touched drugs. My smoking habit soon dropped as well. I was a two pack a day cigarette smoker and my only nourishment was strong Spanish coffee with milk and cookies. When I started the Sufi work, my physical state was deplorable. I had had a serious bout of hepatitis which had almost killed me. Doctors were amazed that I survived. My psychic and physical condition was that of a person years older than I actually was.

With my addictions gone so dramatically, naturally the only thing I wanted to do was the Sufi work. I moved out of Mallorca and travelled with Adnan's group to attend his workshops in all parts of Spain. We did workshops in Madrid, Granada, and in the mountainous Alpujarras region south of Granada. After each workshop, I felt more full of energy and new life. It was an experience I wouldn't have dared dream about previous to running into Adnan in Mallorca, when I had already given myself up for dead.

The workshops in Spain were marvelous. I began to experience a vitality and strength I had never had before. Problems seemed to stop existing, at least as burdens. I remember I did my first fast, three days, in a village in the Alpujarras. It had been less than a month since I had begun the Sufi work and before that, if anyone had told me I would be capable of fasting, I wouldn't have believed it possible, because I had no confidence, no strength ...only fear: a big fear of life and of everything.

Adnan was talking to me about his summer camp program and said, why didn't I come. With intensive work I would change completely and problems would never dominate me again. After the experiences I was having with him, how could I fail to pay him heed? Since then, this is something that never fails: every time I do what he tells me, something wonderful happens to me, a new transformation. I don't know why or how. Adnan seems to know everything that's good for us and even though I don't understand the why or what he tells us, if we do what he says, a wonderful gift is just around the corner. Everything gets better and personal progress and development is enormous.

After I spent almost three months in my first summer camp, the change was frankly startling, so great both physically and psychically. Emotionally, I didn't recognize myself and people I knew couldn't believe the change. Everyone made the same observation, that I was looking and feeling better than at any time of my life, more centered, stronger, serene, etc.

During the winter, Adnan's students in Madrid continued to meet and do Sufi work on a regular basis, and I with them. My body changed even more. I continued to regulate my weight naturally, every muscle and nerve was moving into its proper place as if a marvelous puzzle was being recomposed. Adnan is the one who knows how to set things in their place.

The main thing I did to keep the Sufi process working was to say the prayer (Salat) every day. Not five times a day, not in the beginning, but at least twice. Each time I do it I can feel something happening. Not at all like the ritualistic practices that I did before when I was seeking a spiritual path, prior to my drug experience. I also practiced dancing every day and, with the rest of Adnan's students in Madrid, met twice a week to do Sufi work.

All this helped maintain the results of previous work and kept the process going. Then, when this work, this new energy had been assimilated, I was ready to work with Adnan again and to do exercises directed by him personally. Otherwise, prospects of going further and deeper in the work are slight. At least, that's how I perceive it now. The daily practices away from Adnan feel like maintenance work to me. One thing is certain, the changes that I experience are intense, wonderful and lasting. I never go back to square one. Even in the least encouraging cases, someone may go up five steps, as Adnan says, but will never back down more than two. You never lower yourself to where you were before.

So that's my "update." Barely a year and a half of Sufi work has brought me the most fantastic and incredible changes. And here I am again this summer and all the summers that God permits. This summer I feel even more centered, relaxed and happy, and I feel the more work I do the deeper I go inside myself, more in contact with my true spirit.

I'm stronger than ever. Before, I lived only to satisfy my external senses immediately in a very shallow and self-interested way. I needed constant stimulation from the outside. Now, I'm coming more and more from within. Outside stimulation affects to a very little degree. I feel detached and much more self-confident to do whatever I have to do.

Reflecting on the difference between the other meditation work I used to do, I see that other systems made me feel good when I was in a meditation room environment. When I was out of that environment, I was in a state of tension and nervousness. Such is not the case with Adnan's work. I am constantly coming up with deeper and clearer understanding of myself whether I am with him personally or out in my everyday world in Spain. Maybe it's his special way of combining body work with music and dance and exercise and Sufi meditation. I don't know...yet. I do know that even away from him and the workshop atmosphere I continue to live my life with higher awareness and better perception. My relationships happen on a higher level, unaffected by problems and tensions, as long as I do my personal exercises and the prayer. Cigarettes, drugs, alcohol, even coffee, I just have no desire for them. In fact, I find them rather repulsive. And for that I am very happy with Adnan, that he has taught me how to be content, without resorting to anything artificial.

I thank God for putting Adnan in my life and give thanks to Adnan for helping so much. I only ask that God keep Adnan with us for a long time so that all of us can continue to progress along the Sufi path.

"He who sows the wind reaps the storm." -- Middle Eastern proverb

"Fasting breaks the hold of desire and dispels distraction." -- al-Ghazzali

Bliss After Cocaine

(Excerpts from a talk between
Adnan Sarhan and Roger Stevens)

ADNAN: Maybe you could tell them more about your daughter. They might like to know what happened to her.

ROGER: Daughter Wendy is a beautiful, creative, fun person. But she was enamored of a young man who was injecting cocaine. She wrote bad checks and stole credit cards and such things. She was in jail. And Adnan was in town. I said to Adnan, "I know you cannot make the world good for somebody else, but what can I do for my daughter?"

Adnan said, "The way you teach is to set an example."

I said, "How can I set an example when she is in jail?"

He said, "Then get her out of jail!"

So I went to the judge. I took the prosecutor with me. And I said, "Judge, I have to get my daughter out of jail."

The judge called the guard to bring my daughter in front of him. He said, "You go with your father, but if you do not follow instructions, you go back to jail."

She was afraid to get out because she was afraid that she was so addicted to the cocaine that she would go back to it again. Whether it was fortuitous or by design, Adnan was giving classes and Janet was giving classes at that time, too. We pretty much shut down my law practice for two months. We went to dancing classes in the morning and Sufi classes in the evening and...

ADNAN: And some dinners.

ROGER: And some dinners and some performances. Wendy became a good little belly dancer. I said, "We have to do what Adnan says. You can drink liquor when I drink liquor. You can smoke when I smoke. And you can use drugs when I use drugs."

That was four years ago. Since that time she has not smoked anything. She does not drink. She has given me a granddaughter who is almost three years old now. She has a job. She has a lovely husband. She is a delight.

"Each carcass hangs by its own leg." -- Middle Eastern proverb (Which means that each person is responsible for his own doing. You don't inherit the guilt of other people.)

From Häagen-Daz to Spirit
Julie Elliott
(This was written after Julie quit her addiction to Häagen-Daz ice cream.)

Who am I? I am here.
Longing from the heart,
my eyes are searching, my heart is open,
and then I found you, King of Dawn.
I open my eyes to a new sky, a new earth,
to behold the essence of beauty,
essence of gentleness, essence of purity
that permeates my peaceful soul.
My sky is pink. I am a flower
in a garden of flowers. I am a peach
in an orchard full of peach trees.
I am a star of many constellations.
I am what I am. I am as I am.
My love flows like a stream
traveling to the sea, bringing the coolness
of the mountain's drink
to journey with the river,
to meet the mystery of the sea.
There I exist between the sweet
and the salty. I am where I am.
The spirit comes in waves, sweeping my sand,

my golden shore, and flooding me
with nourishment. My heart opens
like a treasure of gold. My eyes open
to the sea of happiness. Waves upon waves.
Climbing to the mountains high,
to the climax of existence, I grasp
the crisp breath of life that expands my awareness.
I leap into the crystal clear sea of knowledge.
I dive. I swim. With each stroke of pleasure
I go deeper and deeper into the different levels
of consciousness, which mirror the attributes of God.
In that moment, astonished, excited, and puzzled,
I utter the word "Ahhhhh." And then, the bubbles
of experience float to the surface
causing the kindling of the fire on the sea's shore.
Around the blessful fire, the Bedouins of all tribes
are feasting on joy, full of laughter, with feet bouncing
on the pure white sand,
hearts beating to the Master's drum,
reflecting the beat of the invisible heart
that encompasses all. A mystical song rises
from the depth of feelings. To this song,
the women start dancing in circles of light
with colorful veils reflecting the goodness in all.
Veils dancing, dancing, floating, floating
in the moment of drunkenness.
The spirit is alive in the nectar of love,
in the nectar of being. May our spirits unite
in the pinkness of the sunset.

"Beneficial knowledge is the one whose ray of light expands in the mind and uncovers the veil over the heart." – Ibn 'Ata'illah

Barbara Returns to Her Peaceful Self

Barbara Geary

For years I had a vision of myself as free and happy. The vision was always the same: it was of me dancing in a meadow in a long and flowing dress. The sun was warm, the air was soft, and I twirled and swirled with such lightness and grace that I felt like I was floating.

The vision helped to keep me searching. My experience of my life was so far from that vision of lightness and grace. Now I know that the vision is the reality, and that the pain, confusion, problems and seriousness which I invested in myself were simply products of my alienation from myself and the source of true existence.

I think I knew from as long as I could remember that something was "wrong." My life was constricted and heavy, existence was full of effort, and I plodded along, trying to find love and happiness by doing my best to fulfill other peoples' expectations of me. I stacked up hollow academic achievements in an effort to convince myself that I was fine, a winner, the best. And I collected lovers in an effort to convince myself that I was attractive, desirable, lovable, and to fill up the time because time terrified me. I did my best to escape from the fear of facing myself and my emptiness.

When I graduated from law school, I reached a turning point. I was scheduled to come to New York to begin work at a Wall Street firm, and I knew that although it was an enviable job according to the world's standards of money and prestige, it was like a death sentence to me. The idea of spending hour after hour behind a desk, reading and drafting legal documents, was stultifying. How had I ended up like this?

I was also becoming progressively more angry and bitter, and I was frightened by the blackness of my soul. So I went to the University Chapel and there met a man with whom I spent the next year studying theology. It was a step in the right direction, and the beginning of a serious search for a way out of the confusion and emptiness. Although I came to know God at that chapel, much of my time was spent intellectualizing my faith. The more I read and discussed and analyzed, the more baffling it all seemed. I eventually took instruction from a priest and joined the Roman Catholic Church, but as a Catholic I always felt like a misfit. Whoever I was, it was not who the Church wanted me to be.

My life seemed to have reached a stand-still; nothing was happening. I had lovers, smoked a pack of cigarettes a day, and drank a little too much, a little too often. And since I didn't know where I was going, I was going nowhere. With the encouragement of my therapist, I decided that what I needed was the wealth and glamour of New York. So I moved here and began work with the Wall Street firm I had initially turned down. I tripled my income with my new job, but I paid a high price for my impressive salary. I regularly worked until 10:00 or 11:00 at night, sometimes later or even all night, and often weekends as well. I had no friends other than the married men I worked with, and I was exhausted and incredibly lonely. Because my field was international finance, I began travelling a lot, to exotic places like Indonesia, China, Peru, Brazil and Turkey, but I never really enjoyed these experiences because I always felt terrible from too much alcohol and rich food, too many cigarettes, too little sleep and no exercise.

On a trip to Indonesia, I spent a weekend on the island of Bali. I remember laying on a beach at sunset, on the other side of the world, being overwhelmed by the beauty of the natural world in which I found myself, and equally overwhelmed by the lonely, unhealthy, lost and miserable state I was in. I decided on that beach that what I needed was to "settle down," to get married and have a baby, and that this must be the simple answer that had proved to be so elusive. So shortly after I returned to New York, I married a partner in my firm who was recently divorced. I think we both knew that the marriage was a gamble, because we were very different, but we were also both lost souls and I guess we preferred being lost together to being lost alone.

I cried so hard at my wedding that I could barely say the vows. At the reception, I quickly got drunk and have only hazy memories of what was supposed to have been a happy occasion. We went to Egypt for our honeymoon, where we drank ourselves into a stupor every night while cruising down the Nile, and staggered off the boat every morning to visit ruins and tombs. I'm not sure who was more dead, us or the kings.

I became pregnant, quit smoking and drinking, and became absorbed by the happiness of pregnancy and motherhood. But shortly after Rebecca was born, we resumed our extravagant lifestyle of eating out often at New York's best restaurants, drinking every night, and being more and more preoccupied with making and spending money. But no matter how much we had, it was never enough. I was increasingly unhappy and unhealthy. I felt like my life was totally out of control.

I finally insisted that we see a marriage counselor and so began yet another year of therapy. The marriage didn't get any healthier, and eventually ended, but I began to change. I didn't stop drinking completely, but I cut back considerably, and I began to take better care of myself. I quit working as a lawyer and took steps towards pursuing my dream of being a concert pianist. And I began taking dance class with Diane because I have loved Middle Eastern dance and music. Little did I expect what followed when Adnan came to teach Diane's class one day just before Christmas last year.

I think I spent my first year with Adnan in a state of skeptical wonder. I didn't quite trust him and certainly didn't understand him because he was so detached and unpredictable. I loved the fun and comfortable parts of the work, but didn't want to have to look at my life too closely or change too much. I thought I had already been through enough changes. Also, having just gotten out of a miserable marriage, I was looking for fun, not work. I kept retreating, because at the time I was so uncomfortable with myself around Adnan and the Sufis, but there was no place to hide. I felt vulnerable and exposed.

In spite of the powerful experiences I had with the work, I wasn't really committed. I continued to look for happiness in "being in love," and was constantly in a state of emotional turmoil. I continued to drink wine, and I didn't exercise or do the work except at the workshops. A part of me knew that Adnan and the teaching held the answers, but I didn't seem to really want to ask questions. I was always running, too busy, too serious – tense and irritable. Then, when my latest love affair ended a month ago, in the midst of emotional devastation, I turned to Adnan for help, and his love and compassion broke through to me at last. I woke up.

Something has shifted in my perception of the world, as if my vision was out of focus and is now becoming clearer. When I was a child I had a recurring dream in which the world was a giant machine of cog wheels turning out of synchronization, so that the most deafening and frightening grinding and gnashing resulted. And then suddenly the cogs would mesh and the grinding and gnashing would become peaceful silence, and I would be sitting on a curb eating a soda cracker and experiencing the simple peacefulness of the moment.

My world seems to have stopped grinding and gnashing. There is a simple peacefulness to each moment and, miraculously, I seem to be learning how to step into the moment as if into a subtly different dimension – and there, to find the simple, intoxicating pleasure of being alive.

The more I stay in the simple purity of the moment, and in love with my life, the more I find that my life flows from moment to moment like a dance choreographed by angels. Though I am only just beginning the task of truly knowing and being myself, I now trust that the answers do not lie outside myself, but in the spirit within my heart, and that being connected to that spirit is the most important task of my life.

Thank you to Adnan for guiding me to myself by never trying to tell me who I am. There have been times when I wanted nothing more than to please Adnan, to be whoever he wanted me to be, but I couldn't discern who that was. Often the person I saw reflected in the mirror Adnan held up to me was unknown to me because he did not project any identity on to me. He always, with kindness, returned me to myself. I love the way he mysteriously combines exuberance and restraint, strength and softness, intimacy and detachment, playfulness and reverence.

Thank you for being my teacher, Adnan. Thank you for your boundless love, patience and compassion. Thank you for the gifts you are bringing me which are beyond compare: the gifts of my self, my life and the love of my existence. I am finally beginning to experience happiness and it is different and so much better than I expected. It is simple and peaceful and quiet. It has soft edges and melts into itself, and, like love, it is abundant and self-generating.

"If you seek excellence and become excellent, the cosmic power will enhance your vitality, strength and intelligence. If you do not seek excellence, you will never be excellent and you will be no more than gihif, *a fragment of broken pottery." – Adnan*

Tony Becomes a Human Being
Tony Criscuolo, 1980

Another unique summer. In fact, every day is unique as a result of this work and the awareness of the moment it brings. I am fast becoming a human being. It is an evolutionary process here, proceeding at a different pace and affecting diverse aspects for each person involved in this Sufi work.

There is less emphasis on "I" and a deep awareness of the connectedness of all the material in the universe. I feel a part of everyone here and everything around me. Before, I felt a solid, strong separate being. Now there is the taste of unity which comes from the direct experience of the cosmic energy which fuels all of life.

My eyes close and immediately a calm, relaxed state envelops this being--a state of clarity, a feeling of purity and a subtle awareness of deeper inner forces at work transforming the past and opening the joys of the eternal present. The future arrives at its ordained time, the only moment is now. I see so much. Everything is exactly as it should be. It could not be otherwise. Never have I experienced before such strength, such power--not originating from the ego, but beyond ego, rooted in the depths of my being--solid and grounded, yet at the same time flying as free as the wind. A creative energy. And I sense also a deep responsibility for these gifts and that these energies must be applied in the world positively. Still, there is no fear or anxiety, but a faith in the process based on the experiences of the past five years.

I have been saved from a life without deep meaning before I was even aware that the path I was on led there. I am very fortunate. Thanks be to God!

"The soul has an eye as surely as the body has, by which we may know the sovereign truth." – al-Ghazzali

From the Mirage to Miracles
Marianne Damhuis

Until fairly recently, I was living a life filled with 60 cigarettes a day, 20 cups of coffee, lots of business lunches which included red meat, red and white wine and lots and lots of Irish coffees and liquors. I used to pride myself on being able to drink almost any man under the table and drive my car even faster!! I used to travel to Europe pretty often either on business or to relieve the boredom and I would always visit the latest night clubs and restaurants. I was always looking for something new and exciting. I would do wild things. I was rebellious. I used to despise the people I was with, thinking that they were boring and empty. But I did not know how to break out of my lifestyle. The alternative, I thought, was to go for a conventional life and settle down and do conventional things. The thought of that was even worse. I was so bored already and yet I knew there had to be more to life.

Whatever I wanted or thought I wanted, I would go out and get. I could not understand why I was still not satisfied. I thought that it might have been my husband's fault, so I got divorced. Nothing changed. I was still dissatisfied. I started to do workshops like EST and Lifespring which confirmed some of the thoughts I had had. But the main thing they taught me was that I was responsible for my life and I could change anything I wanted to.

My way of reaching for a higher self was through getting involved with politics and human rights which eventually led to my leaving my country (South Africa). I packed 30 years into two suitcases and moved to New York and America.

I remember I had asked a friend a few questions about Sufism, but not too many, as I didn't want to hear about anything that might change my lifestyle too much, and I didn't want to get involved with one of those "spiritual groups" that might upset my drinking and smoking and eating habits. Later, I was invited to Adnan's workshop, but I had no idea what a Sufi workshop would entail. The morning of the workshop, for some unknown reason, I woke up at dawn. I never wake up that early! I got up and put on a tape that someone had given me that I had never played before. It was Middle Eastern music. Not something I usually played. I will never forget watching it get light and hearing the faint strains of this hauntingly beautiful music and feeling something very special inside me and around me. It was very moving. I knew something very big was going to happen.

I had a very powerful experience during the first workshop. It happened just when I had given up expecting anything. Everyone was dancing and the music went on and on for hours. I was beating myself up about not being able to move. I was very critical with myself and very upset because here everyone was doing something I really wanted to do. I was so self conscious I thought everyone was staring at me, especially Adnan, which was the worst because it was very vulnerable for me to be in a position where everyone else knew more than me and I was not the authority. I was the student! All of a sudden, I started to feel this incredible vibration going through my body and my breathing was peculiar. It was like an electric current passing through me. Afterwards, I felt tremendously relieved. I knew something important had happened, and it being my first day, I assumed that was what happened every time. I had got "it". My body felt so relaxed, it was wonderful.

When the workshop ended everyone asked me if I was coming next week. I thought, "That's strange. I've done it. I got IT. Why would I do it again?" When I heard they came back and did this every weekend, I could not quite understand why you would do the same thing twice. Anyway, I was there for part of the following weekend and it was...different.

I remember feeling very spacey in the weeks following that workshop. It was really strange, a kind of a heavy, tired, scattered feeling. My perception of time was a little different and I had difficulty keeping a train of thought. Then Adnan came back to New York to do a few more workshops in June. I did all the workshops. Then I knew that I was definitely "in it" and I had no more doubts about doing the work. I was able to meditate and see the most amazing depths and colors when I shut my eyes. It was overwhelming, such a sense of peace and tranquility and enormous depth, so big there was no concept for how big and deep and wide it was.

In the summer, I went to Sufi Camp in New Mexico. It was lovely. So peaceful. Beautiful days, butterflies, warm, the sky incredible, the thunderstorms amazing. The mountain had so many moods I could watch it forever. It was also nice being with people. I had never been with a large group of people, all eating and cooking together. There was a real sense of community which was new to me. I was shy so I went through some awkward and painful moments of self consciousness, too. I fasted for seven days, which was incredible. I went for a walk and was so high. Every leaf and flower was so bright and clear it was like I was wearing super strength contact lenses...it was like having another sense.

I was only there for two weeks, but by the end of the two weeks, my face had started to change. I looked so much more calm, relaxed and healthy. When I got back to New York, people couldn't believe I looked so good. A friend of mine said before I left that I was going to come back with that "dumb spiritual look", and was he surprised at how full of vitality I looked and how animated I was, without that "spiritual mask" that some people expected me to wear.

While at camp I didn't drink coffee. I didn't miss it at all, but I did get headaches initially. Only when I got back to New York did I realize that this was due to coffee withdrawal. When I got back I could not even face a cup of coffee. And the odd cup that I have had since then has made me feel so wired and ill I could not even tolerate it if I wanted it. The same has happened with alcohol. I cannot take a drink like I used to. My body rejects it and I feel awful even after a few sips.

Recently, when I had a cigarette just to try it again, I felt so nauseous and dizzy I could not smoke it. I also had some Mexican beans and cheese after a workshop and my body rejected it and threw it up. It feels incredible. My body is getting so finely tuned and so sensitive it is like a miracle. I cannot believe that I used to throw all those things into my system and my body actually had to cope with it. I am beginning to respect myself so much I would not dream of abusing myself in the ways I used to.

Five months later, Adnan came back to New York. I could not wait for him to come back and to do more work. I was so excited. It felt like such a long time, although so much had happened since then. I felt like a new person and the past felt like it had happened to someone else. All those years I have been trapped inside my body. I feel it now breaking free. Something has changed and is still changing inside me. Nature is closer, the moon is closer in the sky. I am so much more serene and everything is so much more beautiful. I feel my life and myself purifying. When I am around people who are unaware, who escape in smoke and drink, I feel contaminated. I can't be around that anymore. Also, I am able to contain myself instead of running to some man, relationship, sex, food, alcohol or some other form of escape or outlet.

At times the changes are scary as the old habits and conditioning are being broken down. I sometimes feel I have nothing to replace it with. Nothing physical that is. And sometimes it is like trying to ride a bicycle or to walk a tightrope. I look down and there's nothing physical to support me and I wobble. Then I feel that inner self and spirit that is so strong and I realize that I am absolutely safe. Nothing can harm me. Whatever happens I will be able to cope. Sometimes it feels almost as I should imagine being in the "state of grace" feels. I feel humble and I get an urge to bow down to the ground and pay homage to it. It is something so beautiful and so wonderful. I feel such love. I am so grateful.

"The pleasure of spirit is embedded as trust in the origin of existence and in the heart of man when the man is awake to the true reality."
– Adnan

Marianne Finds Tranquility and New Love
Marianne Damhuis

This summer my body learned a new vocabulary — so many new movements in my dancing, a lot of them learned through Adnan's exercises and movements. It feels like there is a whole new dimension to my physical being. Instead of being upright/vertical, there are all these other dimensions — above, below, to the left, to the right, around me, below me . . . endless like the clouds in the sky moving slowly, separating, forming new shapes, disintegrating, integrating . . . endless, slow, on and on and on. I love the dance, it's like entering a whole new world, each delicious moment and movement leading to the next and the next, each one different and new and then ECSTASY!!! And afterwards a feeling of such indescribable peace and serenity and love.

While I was whirling one day, I suddenly felt something click in and a new energy take over. I was totally out of control and it was moving me around, and around and around. I surrendered. My breathing changed. I was in a very deep state over the next few days. Something had shifted within me. I could see the colored auras and vibrant energy around — everything much brighter than before and everything in nature, including me felt so alive. It felt like I had been transported to another world. I also noticed that even in this state I was still able to communicate with people. This surprised me! Communicating with them did not change my state of being.

I was sleeping less and eating less . . . Bliss! Then I noticed my breathing had gotten deeper and reached deeper parts of my being. And then, another phase where it felt like my heart had been opened and flooded with such intense compassion and such love it almost hurt. I now understand the expression "to love so much it hurts." I was hardly able to contain it. And then I got a flood of realizations, incredible insights into life.

It felt almost like my heart was educating my intellect. Such clarity, such knowledge came from the depths of my being. So many realizations, such a deep knowing, that it surprised me (my head that is). And I would look at Adnan, so full of love, so patient, so gentle, so kind, so giving and it hurt so much I cried and cried. I don't know if this is pain or joy . . . Ecstasy.

It feels like I am being shattered, faced with my ego in so many situations and feeling so totally transparent, naked, a very humbling experience. But also a very, very beautiful experience, accompanied by such peace and love. Thank you, Adnan, for facilitating me through this incredibly beautiful journey. If I have one wish, it is to learn more from you and your example, from which I have probably only perceived a fraction of a drop from the ocean. *Al-hamdulillah*!

"If you fall in the trap of the mirage of life, your thirsty soul will find nothing and you will suffer a great deal." -- al-Ghazzali

Bill Loses 64 Pounds in 60 Days
Bill Hug
(Head of the Dance Department, Florida University)

If I had been asked what I needed and what I wanted before I came to camp, it would have been what goes on here every day. I would, however, not have believed anyone who told me that this would be the case. I came here mostly because of my interest in the spiritual world. I had also hoped to lose a little weight. Well, the spiritual approach is here, but I never thought I'd lose so much weight! To date, I have lost 55 pounds and still have 12 days to go.* This loss of weight has not only changed my present life, but also my potential for the future.

When I arrived here my blood pressure was very high and I was taking pills for it. Now I have not only cut my dosage in half, but have stopped taking the medicine altogether.

Being here has helped me work on myself in many ways. Being used to being in charge and giving orders, my life has been run by the clock. I believe it has been good for me to let up a little, to be told what to do and to live by what is affectionately called "Sufi time." With all the things going on in my outer world, I feel that I'm getting more in touch with my inner one – possibly my essence. The prayer, chanting and whirling have had a lot to do with this.

As to the above and more, I thank God, Adnan and the wonderful people here – those that have helped me directly and those that have just been here.

*By the end of the workshop Bill had lost a total of 64 pounds

"Seek perfection in what you do and finish it with the best of your capability, and God will love you." – *Adnan*

A Night Visit that Changed the Life
Armando Haro, M.D.
(Armando came from Mexico to visit a friend for one night and stayed part of the summer.)

Here, where the daily things of life
are filled with magic,
and the fresh mountain air fills the lungs,
the worldly things come to a halt.
Then a cycle begins which ebbs and flows
beyond time
where there is no past or future,
but only the present, pulsating in the moment,
where the real dissolves,

or in a feeling of certainty,
expands from one to another,
stopping the paths, the trails
that go from heart to heart.
I have arrived by surprise,
one night in August,
moved uncertainly, more by happenstance
than by my own will.
Once past the barriers that my
curiosity imposed,
I have allowed myself to be taken on the
back of a white Arabian horse,
and instead of one night,
it has been one week,
and ultimately, two fluid weeks where,
like someone said,
the seconds pass slowly, slowly;
and the weeks become indescribably long.

This poem captures the spirit elicited by these two weeks of work with Adnan. To recount an experience so profound seems very difficult to me now that the thoughts, feelings, physical sensations, emotions, and philosophies have resulted in something that seems abstract. But within the context of my vivid experience, they have a significance much more concrete.

I have not come here with the intention of needing a personal change. Generally, I believed I had good control of my personal affairs and also had an openness with my feelings. Nevertheless, now that I have done the work with Adnan, there has arisen within me a new conscience that has shown me the necessity of effecting important changes as much inside of myself as in my outside activities, in my physical condition, and my relationships with the world around me.

The first step toward inner peace was the discovery of the potential of breathing and physical connection during the exercises, where I felt a rupturing of internal membranes with a relative gain in flexibility. I began to perceive a change in my health with the cessation of respiratory allergies and lumbar pain, and with improved digestion. Equally evident to me was the absence of a bitter taste in my mouth that I've always had when I wake up in the morning.

A second step was catharsis. During a meditation in the woods, I was crying for a long time without identifying the cause of this suffering. The same sensation continued all day with Adnan's exercises and I could feel a more quiet pain for human misery, for the struggle of power and authority, for injustice and avarice, and for the way I understood how I also contributed to the misery of this world with my attitudes of arrogance and presumption.

After that I entered a new sensation of abundance and harmony that I am feeling now. To discover the universal love as the only premise and value possible may have been the most important lesson during these weeks, and to see clearly the choice of alternatives as a real and definite fact.

Suddenly, I started to feel that which the group calls "energy" and which I had supposed was only a mental suggestion. After reciting a Sura of the Koran, or doing a chanting in the woods, or hearing the drum, I started to feel an internal vibration that in every moment I perceived more strongly. A vibration like gushing water or like a conduction of the force of light throughout my body, a radiation in the atmosphere that was captured more strongly in my chest and hands.

This sensation has been increasing, and during these last days, it comes with extraordinary ease and is provoked by almost anything: a massage, the exercises, the dance, etc. I was surprised with "I Call On You," a song composed by Adnan that we sing and that I thought was a mantra in the matter of energy, but I fell asleep and woke up feeling that my whole body was trembling inside. Other similar feelings have derived from contact with nature, understanding the close relationship and continuation of ourselves in her, some brighter colors, some much more vivid sounds and this spontaneous certainty of our material nature and her latent harmony.

I think this experience with the Sufi work is going to give me change in my life. This sensation of well being has made me see the necessity of abandoning tobacco and alcohol, vices that although they were moderate in me, still stopped me from enjoying this abundance and this joy of simply being alive and in this world.

The techniques of relaxation and physical work are very useful to me now that in my daily routine I am very burned out from my work at night and studies during the day.

A central objective I hope to obtain from this and other future experiences is a better healing power, since in my work as a doctor I am faced continually with an anguished and suffering world that requires care and relief. And the work with Adnan has made me live in my own flesh, which is something that my mind already knew but had not felt: the necessity of integral change of each one of us towards love. Hence, any change on political or social levels that leaves out the spiritual aspect of man is condemned to failure.

Now I leave this place happy and with the clear certainty that I am going to continue this path, because I have seen that it really has heart. New summers will come along with other opportunities to advance towards that light that I have perceived in these two weeks.

I know that the strategy of Adnan's work really allows the possibility of this change, provided that one surrenders in body and spirit to the discipline. In my case, I couldn't omit my skepticism and initial doubt that quickly. Now, knowing the results which have taken place, it is very natural to accept this path of the development of the intelligence (of the heart) as a priority over the way of the intellect (of the brain), which remains in a correspondingly limited place.

I feel much richer now than when I came. But I see the necessity of maintaining this state, of modifying my surroundings in which my responsibility competes and of continuing to learn about life, so necessary for never losing the view that has shown me to this place where every day things mix with magic, and the heart shows the way.

"The soul may see more in an instant than can be written in voluminous books." -- al-Ghazzali

Nancy Wakes Up Under the Bright Sun with a Beautiful Tan
Nancy Andersen

I arrived at camp with few expectations, a tremendous amount of negativity, and a psyche full of worry and fear, guilt and regret, with just enough humor left to keep me afloat. I thought that if nothing else I could lose a few pounds, get a tan, and give my lungs a break from the polluted New York City atmosphere. What has happened and is continuing to happen is a return to a peace and joy that I once knew — and a journey into a state of existence that, while I was always certain it existed, was never in my grasp for more than a moment. I am a veteran of what I call The Long War. Today I am three years clean and sober, after twelve years of drug and alcohol addiction — twelve dark years that included heroin overdoses, international smuggling, a half dozen totalled cars, countless visits to the emergency room, and a steady series of trashed relationships. Somehow through all that I managed to have some semblance of a life, working as an artist, in various bars and restaurants, and running my own business.

From my college days of smoking pot, the Grateful Dead and reading Walt Whitman, I have always been on some sort of spiritual quest, with an internal certainty that there was a connection to the Divine and that there was more to life on this planet than what they were trying to sell me in the pages of Cosmopolitan. Sixteen years ago I did my first training with, and became a part of, a school whose aim was to raise your level of consciousness. It was my first introduction to meditation, chanting, and various techniques and exercises aimed at clearing the psyche of an accumulation of tension, stress and emotional baggage. There was a great deal of theory, but also some very powerful practical work that laid a strong foundation for me and introduced me to a plethora of spiritual teachings and methods, both historical and contemporary.

It was then that I was first attracted to the Sufi Way, but I never came in contact with anyone teaching it. I read Gurdjieff and travelled to Central Asia in search of first-hand experience of the mystic knowledge he described, some of which I came into contact with briefly in Afghanistan. I worked with this school of higher consciousness for many years, on and off, but for all of its good intentions, it was made up primarily of people whose foremost belief was "life in the fast lane" and drugs and alcohol were rampant.

Over the years, as the terror of my own addictions set in, whatever semblance of awakening of my own spirit I had achieved was slowly shrivelling up and fading away inside me. I was dying inside. When, through the grace of God and the miracle of prayer, I finally escaped the deadly grip of substance abuse, a few little sparks began to flicker in the darkness that my soul had become.

At a retreat in upstate New York, I met Marianne, who brought me to my first workshop with Adnan in New York. I don't think he said more than just a few words that first evening but the work hit me like nothing I'd ever experienced before. And that was the whole point — Adnan didn't talk about it and tell us all this theoretical nonsense, he just put us in that state. At that point, however, I still wasn't back to being a fully functioning human being with all my faculties intact. It took another year and a half before I let my resistance down enough to arrive at camp three weeks ago.

My first week was pretty miserable. It was New York City and Wall Street tension withdrawal, combined with the fatigue, headaches, and irritability of caffeine withdrawal — my last holdout for daily doses of toxin. By the end of that week we whirled and it felt like a miniature tornado welling up from the depths of my being — all the tension and anxiety I had been holding on to, just churning up. Staying through the next week when I was ready to run away screaming was just the beginning of the miracle that is unfolding within me day to day. Adnan told me it would get better and that it would happen quickly — and it did, it did.

For the past several years I have felt terminally spaced out. I go through my life, ever-grateful to be free of alcohol and drugs, yet feeling like I'm not quite all there, like I'm not fully present. My experience here at camp is the first glimpse I've had that this mechanical malaise may have a way out. This work continues to awaken in me a freedom, a joy, and an ease in life that had been so deeply buried that I had forgotten the very possibility of their existence. The dependence on caffeine is gone like a shadow in the night. I intended to come here for two weeks. I extended that, first for an additional two weeks, and now for an additional month. Just that experience of changing my schedule to adjust for this, has been a tremendous awakening lesson. To look at what really is and is not of value or importance in my life, and to let go of the false securities. It is first and foremost a restoration of faith, that basic faith that everything really is going to be all right — a faith that I had lost in a deluge of fear.

Today, I feel an energy and a lightness in my being that is beyond description by mere words. The chanting puts me in touch with vibrations of such peace and promise. The diet and exercise make me feel whole and strong again. I feel a confidence and a clarity coming into my life that have been so sorely missing for so long. Just to be able to sit in this room, listening to the soft strains of the music and breathing the fresh mountain air, surrounded by these people; just to be here writing this exercise is a gift of immeasurable value.

"Perfection is the core of existence and it is an ultimate reality in itself. Seek it and the existence will meet you halfway to invest you with perfection." – Adnan

Oh Moment, When I Fell Into Your Prayer, I Woke Unto Your World
James Dillehay

O Moment, where have you fled to? My heart is crying to know you again. You came to me last year unbidden and unexpected. You laid me low with the glory of your splendor. My forehead pressed to the dust before your majesty. My fear of you was my salvation, my ignorance became your grace. I could never earn your visit, how could I hope to win your return?

You showed me the ocean of your being and I longed to dive into the waters of your knowing. When I fasted, the lie of the self became the Truth, and I saw that only you could fast. When I whirled, you made me love you wherever I turned. And when I danced, every cell burned with the ecstasy of your nearness.

As I wander, lost between being and not being, you come and find me and take me by the hand. I look upon your face and I am found. In the heart that only sees the beloved, there is life, and there is love.

What a fool I am that when you called, sometimes I did not answer. How long must I be heedless? Will you not grant me the favor of obedience? What need have I for what I know when your knowing is everything?

When I fell into your prayer, I woke unto your world. When I fell into your world, I woke unto your prayer.

After all is said and done with this flesh, the love of you will be a light, forever pure, forever bright.

"Actions are lifeless forms, but the presence of an inner reality of sincerity within them is what endows them with life-giving Spirit." – Ibn 'Ata'illah

Allah in Spain and the Dancing Nuns
Maria Gracia

My name is Maria Gracia. I'm from Madrid, Spain. In 1956, I started my professional life in the fashion business, first as a model and after as a fashion designer. I owned my own business, a very fashionable boutique in the nicest part of Madrid and afterwards, two others in other areas of town. I had 50 people working for me. After seven years, I sold it all because I became very involved in politics. I went back to the university and took an active part in the student movement of May, 1968, in Paris. Then in 1968, I became a journalist and traveled in Europe for political activities. Later, I specialized in architectural design in Germany and I have worked for a design magazine as a coordinator. At one time, I was the secretary of ADIFAD in Madrid, an international association of design. By 1972, I was the assistant editor of a monthly architectural magazine, "Estructura".

Then in 1975, I left everything I had been doing and started working with a group of ecologists. I became a vegetarian and started doing meditation. I also opened a vegetarian restaurant in Madrid. I then went to Switzerland to take a six month course in Hinduism and to become a teacher of transcendental meditation. I traveled, searching for a spiritual guide.

Now I consider myself a student of Adnan Sarhan. I'm learning with him a wide variety of Sufi techniques. I'm evolving into a new being with the help of his cosmic energy. I felt this energy like an electric current through my body the first time I looked into Adnan's eyes. More and more I feel that energy flowing through me to unify me with the universe. I'm totally dedicated to the Sufi work because I want to be enlightened. I see life as a water wheel always making the same turns and going nowhere and I want to get off and wake up.

I knew Adnan in Madrid in October of 1978. Everybody interested in spiritual life or self-knowledge was talking about him as a great master. Some called him the guru of the drum. Others said he was a Sufi teacher from Baghdad. People were very intrigued because of his great energy and the way he was making people dance with his drum rhythm, even the most serious ones that never used to dance.

The first night I went to his workshop, I saw a president of a big bank dancing madly, moving his body among psychiatrists, psychologists, lawyers, professors and students. I could hardly believe my eyes, but that and more was what Adnan's drum was doing with the most conventional people in town. At first, I was reluctant to go because, at the time, I had just come back from India and I thought I was doing very well with a little bit of chanting and meditation every day. Life was neither bad nor good, as always, but I was hoping that slowly and happily I would come out of the mist inside of me.

My stay in Ganespuri with Muktananda, a spiritual Indian teacher, made me aware of my narcissism and helped to destroy the physical image I had of myself. That image hindered my vision of the other people. All that had been quite painful and I was in the middle of this process when I went to see Adnan. And that was the beginning and the end of everything else. From that moment on, my interior evolution became an all over revolution from within to without. No more quiet and comfortable spiritual life with a little bit of chanting and meditation, but the wholistic adventure of body, mind, senses, psyche and emotions. From the very first day, I got involved in a kind of maelstrom that took away my patterns, habits, beliefs and concepts, and with them my tensions, anguish, stresses, anxieties, griefs, sorrows, my fears, my angers, my repressions, my incapacity to relate equally with the others, my introversion, and all the boundaries that were limiting my life and making my body ill. All that started to happen with the first stroke of Adnan's drum. That stroke changed my life totally. My body and mind reacted to it and the change is still going on after three years. For a long while, I did not even know who I was. I have lost my identity totally. But I always knew I was on the right path and I was never afraid.

Ten years ago, in an accident in Yugoslavia, my car crashed into the sea from a high cliff, leaving my spine and neck badly hurt. Since then, I always had physical pains and headaches and my body became more stiff every day. It was difficult for me to move my neck, and my right arm was starting to become paralyzed. I was getting used to it, but only after going to see many doctors all over Europe. All of them told me that in the end my entire right side would be paralyzed and perhaps I would even need a second operation. I had already had one.

But all that is over now. Adnan's way of fasting made me recover from all those illnesses. And Adnan's exercises and dances have made my body so light and flexible that I cannot recognize it. I feel and dance and move like when I was very young and I'm 48 years old now. I can do headstands, even though I had an operation on my neck which had been broken during the accident. It took me two years to accomplish that, during which I tried every day until I did it.

Now, I'm following Adnan through America most of the time and I go to Spain a couple of times a year. In Spain, people are asking for Adnan. They want Adnan to come back. They remember his workshops and they would like to study with him, but the majority can not economically afford to go to America. The first year more than twenty people followed him to the summer camp in the State of New York, but they were doctors and psychiatrists and had to go back to work at the hospitals.

Adnan went to Madrid for a weekend and stayed eight months because the people liked his work so much. First, he was at the University of Madrid. From there, we traveled with him to Valencia, where he had been invited by a group of psychologists. Then we went to Granada where he played his drum in the famous music room of the Alhambra Palace. The Alhambra Palace is one of the greatest buildings that·is left from the Arab glory in Spain.

From Spain, he went to Paris, invited by a group of experimental psychologists, and many Spaniards followed him. Every weekend, we left Spain on Thursday for Paris, to meet other people from London and other parts of Europe. Then we came back on Sunday after the workshop. People from Bilbao, an industrial city in Spain did the workshops and also people came from Ibiza, the famous island on the Mediterranean. It was quite an extravaganza. We followed Adnan everywhere. He was becoming as popular as a bull-fighter.

While in Madrid, he was invited to a seminary to take part in the ceremony for the graduating priests. Adnan played the drum. The nuns and priests danced with Adnan's drum, even the very old nuns danced frantically and the young priests, too. Then, Adnan taught them the chanting of *Allah* and continued to drum. It was beautiful to see the nuns and the priests and all the people invited, perhaps as many as a thousand, chanting *Allah, Allah, Allah*. I was looking at that and suddenly I had the impression that I was witnessing an historic event. In very Catholic Spain, in a Catholic convent, the name of *Allah* was invoked by the nuns, the priests, and the Catholics. It was the first time after five centuries since the end of the Arab rule in Spain that the name of *Allah* was in the mouths of the people. I saw it as a message of love and light.

I was resentful when Adnan first started teaching the prayer. The other Spaniards and I used to say, "We'd better be careful because if we start doing the prayer, we may end up Muslims without even noticing it." But the prayer becomes a way of life and I really notice it. The prayer is like Adnan's drum: it goes into you and erases every trace of the mask that the circumstance of your life has put on you. You get purified by it. It makes it possible for you to contact the Absolute. From this contact, darkness disappears and one knows more and more about oneself. The prayer is the means of changing and is the key to opening ourselves to love, but not to the emotional love, to the true love. Love is the unifying stuff between us and the others, between us and the universe and between us and God.

I'm happy to have Adnan as a teacher, and he is the perfect teacher for me. I have faith in the work he does and I feel this is the work I need. But my faith is not a blind one. It is alive, and I renew it every day by being open to receive his transmission without any doubts to interfere in the alchemical process that makes the relationship between teacher and pupil effective. But I'm not a fanatic and I never will be. I'll keep my discrimination ever growing with the other qualities that the work has developed in me, like flexibility, adaptability, stability. I feel a new intelligence is growing in me with the help of this energy and Adnan's skillful training and sometimes eccentric wisdom. He is a man from a different culture, from a different state of consciousness and spirit. I don't understand him all the time, but I have learned to accept him and to surrender to him within, while keeping total responsibility for my physical life and my spiritual growth.

This very unique and easy quality is at the core of all his teachings and makes it so different from the others. He develops in his students these two states: freedom or contraction and submission or expansion. That is also the key to his dance meditation: movement of the body leading to stillness of the mind and the use of rest and activity, just like the rhythm of the universe. To follow him in this way, we become strong like a lion and innocent like a dove.

Three years ago I was insecure, anxious, angry, fearful and unhealthy. Now, I am happy, serene, healthy and strong; and who knows, perhaps I will end up being enlightened.

"Intelligence is a light in the heart which distinguishes between truth and vanity." -- al-Ghazzali

"We should take ourselves no more seriously than they take us." -- al-Ghazzali

Seeing Without Glasses
Lincoln Wildner, M.D.
(Excerpt from a talk between Adnan Sarhan and Lincoln Wildner, M.D.)

ADNAN: I have seen definite progress in you through the time. And that progress has been going higher and higher. In fact, the beginning of that was the experience you had in Virginia. That was one of the highest I have ever seen in the power of change which took over in you. You completely looked like another person, immediately. It was during the morning work.

LINC: Yes, I remember that very well.

ADNAN: We were out in the open.

LINC: I would be glad to describe that. This was at the completion of a five day workshop at a retreat in the countryside in Virginia near a small place named Syria.

As I said, this was the final day and we were working out in the open doing exercises, calisthenics and so on. Just before this Adnan said, "I want you to observe those trees on the hill over there. Just keep looking at them with half closed eyes. Just keep observing them. Do not look too closely. Take in the whole field of view."

While we were observing the trees there were slight breezes. The trees were about half a kilometer away. I remember that I felt as if I were a tree myself. It is very difficult to explain. When the trees were moving with the breeze, gently one way or the other, I felt instinctively like I was a tree or a branch moving with them. There was no conscious effort.

After we had done that for a while, Adnan asked us to get up on our feet. And we were to do a special exercise with our eyes half closed. We were to take four slow steps and then we were to breathe in and think the word *Allah*. We were to do this many times. We were to keep our eyes open just enough so we would not run into each other or fall into a ditch.

I was totally absorbed in this exercise. I remember hearing the sound of a little stream. So I thought to myself, I had better cheat and open my eyes or I might fall into the stream. So I opened my eyes just enough to see where I was. When I opened my eyes, something very astonishing was happening in my vision. I noticed my vision was more clear than it had ever been in my life. I could see trees and branches very clearly a long distance away. I could read the license plates on automobiles in the parking lot quite a distance away. I remember that I was very astonished and I felt for my eyes. I said, "I am not wearing my glasses. What is happening?"

I had been very near-sighted since I was a child of ten years old. I was so near-sighted that without my glasses I could just barely see that there were automobiles there. I could not read anything on them. There I was reading license plate numbers at a distance away without my glasses. I looked around further and I could see tree branches. I could see a building, all the wood on the building and the doors, without my glasses. This was the first time I could do that without my glasses since before I was ten years old.

I remember I got very excited. I was running around and tears were coming out of my eyes. When you have had bad vision like I had for so many years, that was a miracle. I remember running around and telling people, "I can see! I can see!" I ran up to Adnan and I think I embraced him.

I remember I had a feeling or a lot of energy like I was ten years old again. I just wanted to run around and run around. Everyone was ready to quit and I wanted to play hide and seek.

We went into the house to get the last meal for the group. I remember that inside the house the air had a blue tinge to it as if it was electric or something. It was very light, as if in a vacuum or something. My friends at the workshop could tell something special was going on. They said that my eyes were shining in a very unusual way. They said that it looked to them like I could see right into them.

Then we went back to Washington. I was so full of energy that I almost wanted to run back rather than to drive back.

There was another evening workshop in Washington that we were going back to. This feeling of tremendous energy lasted several hours even after the workshop stopped. I was still running up and down in the building like a little child. I think the energy must have been infectious. You remember the old whirling record you had?

ADNAN: Yes.

LINC: *Allah, Allah, Allah..* Everyone was whirling real fast. That was fast whirling we did there, until one fat man fell

49

down and sprained his ankle. He thought he had wings. Being a doctor, I felt I had to take care of him. After I took care of the man with the sprained ankle, my feeling of so much energy went down. But I have never lost the recollection. Many times since then, from chanting, from saying suras, even from drumming, I get briefly similar feelings, such clarity from my vision.

"The most ignorant of all people is the one who abandons the certitude he has for an opinion people have." -- Ibn 'Ata'illah

Finding the Essence
Tamsin Murray

I was a thin, tense, grey shadow with the glazed look of nervous exhaustion in my eyes when Adnan and the Sufi people first saw me. I smoked 20 to 30 cigarettes a day for eight years, drank occasionally for catharsis and took drugs because it was a way to stay on the same level as my peers, otherwise I just felt lonely. I favored sarcasm, irony and cynicism.

The simple-mindedness of more spiritually aware friends of mine was a quiet joke. I needed complex situations and smoky nightclubs with the grey haunted faces of painted transsexuals. And this attraction to destructive black powers mirrored the blackness of my lungs, the grey of my tongue and the stench of my hair.

But when I came to the Sufi workshop, I didn't bring my cigarettes because I had a strong feeling ever since I saw the ad in the "Voice" that I wouldn't need them anymore, that I would change.

I didn't know then anything about Adnan and his "Shattari method." Idries Shah had not written anything about Shattari, or drumming for that matter.

At the workshop I slunk into a corner and watched Jolinda dancing, half wondering whether these people were going to be wishy-washy. They were too friendly, too colorful and far too happy to have any intelligence that I knew of. I spied Adnan walking around in his white clothes. He looked like the teacher, probing everyone.

The first exercise I remember was getting in a big circle and following his movements. About ten minutes into the exercise, I didn't care whether the people were good or bad or wishy washy. I just moved with the sense that this was the best thing and I wasn't leaving it.

Adnan came up to me after the work and told me to look in the mirror. I would not look in the big mirror, it was too public. So I made my apologies and moved to the bathroom. The door was shut. I was alone and I stood at the mirror. I studied my face. What was I looking for? I wasn't too sure. He had just told me to look. My face was open.

After that weekend, Adnan did not return to New York for four months. But in that time I went to Diane's classes and danced. I had one half of a cigarette and one night of drinking in the four months he was away. The cigarette tasted as if I was licking out the lid of a bin left out for two weeks on an East Village street corner. I may as well have. In fact, that might may have been a more pleasant experience.

In the past when I have tried to give up cigarettes, my will would work to push me past the taste to getting hooked again. This time it couldn't do it. One puff of that cigarette and I ran to clean my teeth and get rid of the taste quickly. My will was no longer working for the destructive side, at least not on the level of taste and breathing. It was working for someone else. Adnan, I think. Even my ex-boyfriend could not sway me. And he continued to offer cigarettes to me each day, blowing smoke in my face and smoking while we ate. All my friends smoked but now there was a rift between us. The only solace from the existence I had led and was about to cut was Diane's classes.

When Adnan did come back I told him and he was pleased. But this was only the first step. Eight years of abuse means quite a few years of detoxification, elimination, reorganizing and strengthening. My first summer camp was pretty much dominated by the theme of cleaning up. My abuse had expanded so much that it embraced not only my lungs but my environment. I was a slob.

I was a tragic mess before Sufi work and the summer taught me how to repair the damage. My childhood vision of what life was supposed to be was reawakened as a tangible and workable reality.

I remember writing words to this effect years ago that the sign of a true master is the ability to strip an individual down to the very core that exists within him and then rebuild the individual again in accordance with the essence of that human core. I used to imagine what it would be like meeting and having a Sufi teacher. I didn't know then that the process would involve a whole community of like minded people and a teacher that commands and creates unconditional respect for what is inside you and sees past the stupid saboteurs, who try to deflect the power of this whole experience elsewhere. Part of the effort is learning to be willing. And like in the Persian tales, the growing intimacy with God is like being in love and to realize that *Allah*, God, whoever, is in love with what's inside us makes the experience of every moment a yearning to be eternally united. It's the healthiest passion I've ever experienced.

Now I could never go to a nightclub for sustenance, never touch a cigarette, a drink, a joint, never sit in a room with people on drugs without feeling physically nauseated by it. I could never wish to trade in the Sufi work for a life that condones this kind of inhumanity, and I never ever want to wish it upon others to continue such habits.

The bravery, the clarity and the purity that I possessed as a child has slowly returned. It wasn't as if these qualities had been kidnapped as I had believed previous to the Sufi work. On the contrary, what would possess them to want to cohabit with misery, apathy and chemical poison? That the good qualities return at their own convenience is a marvel to witness and a blessing.

I could launch into a thousand analogies describing the natural development of what happens when you begin to deny negative things and embrace the positive, but I'll stick to the smoking story. Okay, once upon a time I smoked, then I did the Sufi work, and then I stopped smoking. Thank you, Adnan.

"He is alone wise who is a master of himself and the ignorant is the one who is a slave to his desires." -- Muhammad

Kaye Finds Peace of Mind
Kaye Webb

Overall this summer has moved right along very smoothly like a flowing brook winding its way around stones and obstacles but still remaining gentle and free. But today this brook of mine ran head on into an enormous rock wall that wouldn't let me pass until I had turned in the right direction towards God. Perhaps distress is an extra bonus that God lays in our path as a test to see if we have learned anything these summers at Sufi camp. Will we use what we know to change the negative to positive or will we just indulge in the negativity? We are so fortunate to know the chanting, the breathing, the Koran and the exercises to help us in times of distress. If Adnan could teach everyone in the world or if each of us could pass a little of this knowledge on to others, just think how this world could be — like heaven on earth.

This work has been a blessing that helps me through every aspect of life: helps me to always remember the source – where we came from, where we are going and not to get stuck in ruts along the way, and not to take life so seriously but to laugh, to enjoy the life, to be accepting and find amusement in situations instead of complaining, worrying, becoming tense and creating problems.

Every summer is full of transformations and change. I never leave here the same as when I arrive. Through the discipline and practices of the work, I gain inner strength which is a great source of comfort and contentment in this world in which we live.

Thank you, Adnan, for a gentle yet extremely powerful summer.

"Seek the moment and the time will entertain you, and you will see marvels beyond anything that you know." – Adnan

Dianna Realizes She is a Masterpiece of Creation
Dianna Christenson, 1993

When I came to your summer workshop in July I was looking for a miracle. Having recently been diagnosed with M.S. (multiple sclerosis) of the rapidly progressive kind, my doctors suggested that I do whatever I could this summer before I became totally disabled. It had been over two years since I last attended one of your workshops – my finances were limited, but my thinking was obviously even more limited! When I received this grim prognosis in July, my thoughts turned immediately to you, summer camp and the Sufi work. I remembered how I had such trust in you, how the work had helped me become more positive, but also how I ran like a terrified animal from the changes which were beginning to occur as a necessary result of this work. After all, I had had so many changes in the past few years I wasn't at all sure I could handle more. But now, I could no longer run. I couldn't even walk without difficulty and the possibility of becoming totally disabled hung ominously close to my being. When I called you at camp and you told me to just come and I would be fine, I felt such a sense of relief and complete trust that I wondered why I had ever feared or doubted this process which would probably save my life.

My boss at the University of Hartford was more than understanding. He arranged for me to have an extended sick leave with pay and gave me the round-trip airline ticket to New Mexico. I had already made up my mind to take my vacation time and, if need be, borrow the funds to come to the camp for a couple of weeks, but I never would have dreamed that once I made the commitment to come to camp everything would fall so perfectly into place. The miracle had begun. In a few days I landed in Albuquerque, walking unsteadily with my cane and carrying more emotional baggage than any airline could handle. When I arrived at camp I felt like I had come home — weary and broken, but with the assurance that this was where I was supposed to be and I would be accepted into the "family" in spite of the pathetic state in which I arrived.

I knew that I had started a wonderful healing process when I made the commitment to come to camp, but I was not prepared for the incredibly rapid way the process took hold. Within a few days I had totally discarded my cane, was hiking, dancing and whirling as if I was in the very best of health! What was even more meaningful for me was the reconnection I felt with spirit and the sense that a higher, more developed and integrated intelligence was at work which I knew could not, by its very nature, lead me in any direction that was not for the well-being of myself and those around me. Tears which I had repressed for years began to flow freely — not in sadness or despair, but in pure joy and the beauty of the moments as they unfolded before me. This was a total happiness I had never even dared to experience before – and it was real. When the dark clouds of fear would try to overshadow the beauty of the moment, I had only to immerse myself in the work so that which lies already perfect within could develop. Then all fear, anger and negativity would disappear, and I knew my life would never be the same again.

After I had been at camp for three weeks, I received word that my daughter had been critically injured in an automobile accident. I would have to leave camp and go to New York to be with her. Ordinarily, this would have caused an excessive amount of stress and activated all the M.S. symptoms, leaving me weak, confused and not very mobile. I left with the heartfelt prayers and good wishes from Adnan and all the beautiful people here at camp and I knew that not only would my daughter recover completely, but that I would also be well throughout this ordeal. My daughter astonished her doctors with her rapid recovery, I did not develop any of the dreaded symptoms of the M.S., and I knew that I had to come back to the fountain for more healing. I knew now that the work was indeed saving my life.

My second few weeks here at camp proved to be even more powerful than the earlier session. I now had the understanding that all I need to be truly alive, well and productive lies within this beautiful alchemical process Adnan so generously offers to those of us who will accept the gift. Why, I had even started working on my long neglected drawing and sculpture again which was a miracle in itself!

I thank you, Adnan, from the depths of my soul, for allowing me to come home, even after I strayed from the path. I thank you for your kindness, your gentleness and your unconditional acceptance of those of us who have wandered and been lost in the illusion of life. But most of all, Adnan, I thank you for your tremendous spirit which inspires and renews, and for your infinite wisdom that leads us to the reality and to the miracles we each need to realize, that we truly are the masterpieces of creation.

I came looking for a miracle and found so very much more. May I never wander alone and lost again.

"Let your spirit usher you to the hidden world of time and its reality, beauty and charm will be revealed to you." – Adnan

Laurie Abolishes Smoking, Drinking, Drugs and Coffee
Laurie Temple

I started my personal journey to change my life for the better in 1979 as a broken person practically ready to give up the battle — addicted to alcohol, nicotine, caffeine, and other things. In just one amazing weekend on the Island of Ibiza, Spain I quit all these intoxicating habits. I shall never forget sitting in that cafeteria after Adnan's workshop, trying to inhale the tobacco and drink the beer and I just could not take it into my body; and that is a person who had been drinking beer nonstop, daily! I was shocked and asked Adnan what was going on and he replied simply, "The positive energy has replaced the negative energy."

So much water has flowed under the bridge since that momentous turning point in my life. In those days, I just could not sit still and hold a conversation or look into another person's eyes. I was so filled with confusion, nervousness and pent-up emotions. To observers, it must have seemed as if I had "ants in my pants." I would sit and jump up, sit and jump up, run around the block, sit at the cafe and order something, say "hello" to my neighbor, then immediately jump up and run around the block again, pursued by a host of inner tormentors.

I still see Adnan so vividly sitting at the same outside table, after the workshop, day after day, in his shining sunglasses, just sitting there calmly, still, observing. And I could not understand this "phenomenon." As I rushed past, nervously, on one more circuit of the block, I just could not understand how anyone could sit still like that for so long, and not just once, but day after day! So on one occasion I brought my speeding vehicle of a body to a screeching halt opposite this mysterious man and asked, "What are you doing, why are you doing it?" And he replied, again so simply and to the point, "This is one of the best experiences: to sit and observe, to witness life. Also, to see some people rushing around in circles, like chickens without heads." "Oh, I see," I said, rushing off painfully to join the other chickens.

Now as I sit here writing this report, myself so calm and detached, observing and feeling every finest detail, within me and without, I am open-eyed and open-hearted. I am literally a new person, quite reborn. This work with Adnan is simply extraordinary. The changes are so rapid.

I remember once telling Adnan a dream I had of him riding a large motorcycle with me on the back, racing along, the wind blowing our white scarves into the air. And he said to me, "This is the Sufi work. It is the rapid method and will take you to your destination like on a rocket. The other ways are like traveling by donkey."

Adnan is the greatest of guides. I love being here so much and doing this work. It is the most passionate and enjoyable way of life and the greatest of challenges — to break down one's ego, that cunning, mischievous, dangerous separator and divider, to experience an ever-growing, expanding, merging with life, swimming joyfully in the waves of creation.

With this Sufi work I feel myself grow up from moment to moment. I still feel as if my life depends upon it as I first did in 1979, because it is feeding my spirit and soul and is such a joy — to change and grow, to laugh and enjoy one's growth, to feel profoundly connected to God, to Creation, to each of my friends here, all connected in the spirit, in the moment. *Al-hamdulillah* and thank you, Adnan.

"When comfort comes from the spirit, you could be at the North Pole and you feel as if you are in heaven." – Adnan

"When comfort comes from material, you could be in heaven but you feel as if you are in a stinking swamp with a million rotten dead mice." – Adnan

Christina and the Wine of God
Christina Casanova

January, 1991. I have spent the last 40 years of my life in the search for meaning and purpose in my life. I took many roads in my journey, looking toward the outside to fill the underlying basic anxiety and empty feeling inside: the Catholic Church, marriage, psychoanalysis, three advanced degrees, food, alcohol, relationships, etc.

In 1985, after a big depression in which I felt I was literally dying, I felt a spiritual awakening. My journey led me to read many books on esoteric and spiritual traditions. I attended numerous trainings, such as Neurolinguistic Programming, Reiki, Imagery, Astrology, Buddhist meditation and many others. I felt that every training and workshop was a piece of a puzzle, and now I realize that Adnan's work integrates all the pieces, the body, the mind, sound, meditation, diet, exercise, ritual, and movement with the utmost simplicity.

The first night of the workshop, I felt entirely at home. The atmosphere of non-judgment and acceptance was evident in everybody present. I have a very stressful, busy job as a psychologist/administrator in the New York City School

System. I came to my first night pretty stressed and left after three hours in a state of harmony and peace. I decided to take every workshop and managed to change business and personal plans to attend. I intuitively felt that this work had a powerful transformative force.

After one month and over 100 hours of your work, I feel very much at peace. I have experienced more peace, love, harmony, power than at any other time in my entire life. Many are the things I am discovering and appreciating daily, like great esteem for my body. In doing the exercises and meditations, I felt the ills of my body vibrate with light and my body and space surrounding it fill with peace and harmony. I realized that for 40 years I was looking to the outside to fill what I already have inside, but never felt. As this happened, a sense of control over food and drink began to develop effortlessly; not out of a "must" but a new sense of love and respect for my body. The realization that God is the only reality, and that my body is a "form" to carry the wishes of the spirit, has resulted in a very joyful attitude towards taking care of my body, to be able to express more fully the spirit.

The exercises and meditations have helped my wandering mind experience for the first time the beauty of being present, in the moment. One of the days during meditation I lost track of time, space and boundaries. No consciousness of the self, just void, but a void that was full and pregnant. I thought afterwards that that is how death must feel, how heaven must feel.

A sense of self confidence that is new is growing more and more in me, as if the emotions of fear or frustration are not in my reality as much as before, as if a loving sense of trust in God is present and filling my life.

I want to thank you for the gift of the Sufi work. It has given me the hope to continue on the journey that has made me experience the presence of God in a joyful, non-serious and non-stressful way. The Sufi work is the difference between faith and knowledge. I know that I have begun to know and experience the spirit. Thank you, Adnan, for what I consider the greatest gift: an introduction to myself.

March, 1991. Since my report last month, many more "happenings" and shifts in perception have occurred in my life. I am beginning to have the impression that instead of doing the work, the work is being done to me. Here are some of the stories of my journey of transformation.

My work as a psychologist for the New York School System requires that I give workshops to clinical and pedagogical staff. This usually means two to four days preparation for each presentation. Last week was particularly busy in our office and I had no time for preparation until the night before. I came home rather tired from the office, at 9:00 pm, ready to take a shower and work all night on my presentation. Then I remembered your telling us that the intellect alone causes confusion. I decided to trust the Intelligence of the Heart. Instead of figuring any strategies, I chanted *Allah hu* with the tape, and went to bed listening to another Sufi song. The next morning I chanted *Allah hu* again and asked the spirit to guide me in the workshop. My presentation was very creative and unusual and was very well received by everybody. I was asked to come back and to share the "model" that had developed!

Norma and I bought tickets to a Broadway show early in January for February 15. As the date approached, I realized that we had Sufi class that evening. I was torn between keeping my word to my friend and not disappointing her, and my desire to be at Sufi. My body literally cringed at the thought of sitting in the theater, as if it refused to do something it did not want. I cancelled my date, paid Norma for my ticket (a small way to thank her for her graciousness) and went to Sufi that night. As we were doing the Sufi dance, I realized that I was through with being a passive observer of life. From now on, I am an actor, I am the life, I am the dance.

At the end of our monthly staff conference, my friends waited for me for our usual trip to the local bar. "Ready for a drink?" asked Ruby. "I don't drink anymore," I answered. These words came out of my mouth clear and certain. Did I say that? I asked myself, realizing that I had not had a drink for at least a month. Adnan's work has helped me find what's real, dropping all the other crutches.

After doing Adnan's work for two months, I have come to expect the unexpectable as normal. I arrived Monday morning to my cluttered desk, looked at the five To-Do lists, filled with deadlines, projects, meetings, letters to be answered, workshops, etc., etc. What was the difference? My attitude towards work! All these papers, projects, deadlines that filled my time looked to me, this Monday morning, thoroughly irrelevant. I felt as if there had been a real shift in the axis of my being. Being and discovering my real self meant I no longer needed to put meaning into what was meaningless. I AM real. I AM. That's all!

Last night I whirled for the first time. I felt I was whirled right into the arms of God. As the music went faster and faster, an overwhelming feeling of joy possessed my body and soul and I heard the spirit whisper softly in my ear, "Welcome home."

Adnan, you will always have my gratitude for providing us with the tools to reach the spirit and what is real in us. I feel that in finding you I have won the "cosmic lottery". You told me this is just the beginning. I look forward to continuing the journey with you and the Sufi family.

"God lives in the moment, and if you get in it, you will be with God in the house of God, and He will give you cosmic candy unknown by human beings." – Adnan

What is Happening to Me?
Dimitri Athanasiou, 1983

Nine months ago, just a few days before Christmas, I was laying on the sofa-bed of my living room, in my NYC apartment. It was around 7 o'clock on a boring Sunday afternoon which I had to go through alone since my wife was in Miami visiting her parents.

I was thinking of rolling a joint and spending my night at the movies, so I leaned from my bed trying to reach the "Village Voice". With a long slow stretch--oh, if I knew what those stretches would do to me later--I reached the newspaper to discover with great disappointment that it was last week's and the new one was sitting on the table, at the other end of the room. It's a good thing that the good movies stay in NYC for a few months so I didn't have to move. Looking through the pages I stopped at the body-mind-spirit section which I had been checking often the previous few months, just to see what kind of gurus were in town and what they had to propose for my salvation.

Oh yes, this is a good one: Adnan Sarhan, the Sufi. I thought he would be a good break from all those long haired and long bearded Indian yogis with their ethereal clothing and funny accents. Plus the show was only a few blocks away from my home and it cost $3 (cheaper than the movies). So I decided to spend my night there.

Next morning, I quit my job and I did all the 15 day workshop.

After that I did the three weeks in Hawaii.

Then it was time for the summer camp, so I caught a plane and there I was underneath the bluest sky on the earth, between the greenest trees in the world, shaking my hips, saying a Moslem prayer, fasting or eating two plates for lunch and three for dinner (not to include the peanut butter sandwiches in between). What has all this done to me? Two months now? Is that what you are asking?

Ha! And you think it's so easy to answer! Well, to be honest I don't exactly know. Yes, yes, I could tell you about the changes and the wonderful time. About the moments of bliss and those of deep religious experience, that I don't smoke anymore, I don't need drugs or alcohol, I don't worry about the future or my relationships, I'm open and I love everybody here. I even get pleasure washing the pots at night! Also, about the shaking and the crying and the release from so many complexes. I could tell you about the unbelievable sunsets, the moon and the stars, the most beautiful wild flowers, the magic forest with the toads who sit still in your hand while you are meditating.

But please, can you tell me, what's happening to me?

"A man who knows will not waste his time in any work when his spirit is not part of it." – Adnan

From Hell to Eternity
Mary Anne Bachia

Yesterday I did a head stand without anyone holding my legs for the first time in my life. I've 30 years behind me and I'm just starting to live. There's a wonderful connection in seeing the world upside down and what's happened for me in my life this summer.

What did I used to be like? Well, I've been through years of self destruction and abuse. I used to be a punk rocker and hung out with people who called themselves Hell and Rotten, Excessive, Suicide, Dead Boys, Gun. I hung out with Hell's Angels who share their girlfriends out to friends sometimes. I sold myself to men, shot drugs, drank, smoked and hated fiercely - mostly men who I had an abusive way with. If they didn't abuse me, I'd abuse them. I had years of treating myself like trash and believing that was all I was worth. I was really flaky and scared and weak and tried to hide it with a hard exterior.

My salvation was banging on the piano and screaming and living in New York where people were broad minded enough to call it "powerful music". I misinterpreted anger for devotional passion, and drama for love. I was never satisfied, I think, in all my life. I was always searching. Even as a child I was never satisfied with the love that came my way. I guess I always felt such deep love and devotion and never connected with where to steer that energy in a solid way, so I could feel the love grow from the inside, instead of striving to find it in someone else.

This summer I can feel the different person I am from who I used to be. I see situations and I see the way I used to react in them and now I react differently. It's like having two heads. Whole parts of my behavior seem to be missing. Where's that joke I would say right here or why am I not jumping up and down on a table?

I try to play the piano and nothing comes up. I don't need the rage anymore and haven't learned to express this peace through music yet, although singing the Koran has been incredible for me. Sometimes I actually feel my heart vibrating. The peace is intense. Dancing has changed for me, too. As Adnan said to me once, "Last summer you couldn't move." Now, my body feels like a river flowing through dreams of music, beautiful, deep and profound.

The head stands. Well, the greatest beauty I feel changing my entire being is in seeing the world from the opposite direction from what I've been used to. I realize that with all the negativity I've lived through I've been looking at my life through those dirty windows. I see periods of time, always through my negative experiences of those times. Well, now I realize that if that's what I dwell on, that's what I get. My past has become much more of a story for me and an example of the miracle of strength of the spirit in a human being to survive being stomped on by a monster truck, one of those with huge wheels that stomps on cars, and the spirit rises up glowing. *Al-hamdulillah*!

Sometimes I feel my ego want to attach itself to my past and I flare up, feeling like moving back to New York to be a jazz musician barging around all over the place. Having attached myself to being an artist for a long time I have enjoyed that label in the past but what comes up for me is that it doesn't matter what I do in my life as long as the attachment of my self-worth isn't there.

The spirit is all that matters. That's all there is to life, that and devoting myself to love. The immensity of my love is new for me to recognize and I'm astonished. Finally, after all my life so far, I'm learning to truly love *Allah* with all my heart and be inside that love instead of asking or hoping for anything in return.

While watching the stars at night, laying out in awe of the universe, I realize more and more profoundly that I am just a vessel through which this beautiful love energy flows. We come from ashes and leave the same. All we have is the generosity of Allah to give us life at all.

Adnan, I don't think I can put in words all the love, trust, beauty and peace I feel towards you. How warm and gentle my heart throbs for the essence of life you help us to see. Thank you. Allah's blessings upon you.

"To be just to one's inner soul means to be purified from all the inner impurities including low desires, anger, lust, hatred, greed, pride, revenge, etc." -- al-Ghazzali

Tracey Lost Her Love for Smoking
Tracey Fischer

I've smoked for eleven years, never under a pack and a half a day. At different periods I smoked even more. In the past year it became more and more evident I needed to quit. Maybe I was getting sick more often or I must have started feeling more and more miserable. I quit and started several times and each time I started it hurt more and felt worse and tasted horrible. I really didn't know how I was going to stay away from them. I really felt that "Once a smoker, always a smoker." I just couldn't see me not smoking even though I hated it! I lived on coffee and cigarettes for years. Food didn't matter. I would be perfectly content with a pack of cigarettes and a refillable cup of coffee.

The first workshop I went to, I met Adnan and Sharon at the door. I hadn't heard anything about Adnan or the workshops, but I was interested in belly dance and had had a vision of being surrounded by Middle Eastern music and dancing, but not necessarily Middle Eastern people. Well, a week later, I told a hairdresser friend about this vision, and he insisted I meet Azra (whom he had worked with previously). We tried for a couple of weeks to get a hold of her and couldn't. Then finally I came home one night and there was a message from her about a workshop five blocks away and for only five dollars. What a deal! That was all I could afford on extra curricular activity.

Well, like I said, they were waiting in front. Adnan barely spit out hello before he was telling me I would not only quit smoking but he would make me quit and all the other vices, too, like drinking, drugs, coffee, etc. Not a particularly great opening, but he was allowed to believe whatever he wanted!

So up the elevator we went. I was definitely nervous now. These people were too beautiful and hip looking, too. There was no way they were all straight. Into the room. Oh God, it was like a rainbow gathering. Everyone in their proper fashions in their circles. Nothing's more intimidating than beautiful women sitting in their circles. I definitely would never be one of them. And I've thrown out my granola garb for the last time. This is New York City, not Boulder or Berkeley!

Sharon pushed me right up front for the workshop. I adored all the breathing and arm movement, and the dancing was wonderful. I also couldn't believe Adnan when he said I would be able to dance like the girls in the middle without years of practice. I knew that I wanted to dance like that and somehow it was okay for these women to dance so freely in front of this man. Whoever he is, he's not stupid. That's for sure!

It was a nice walk home that night. I smoked a cigarette to prove his spell didn't work. It felt good lighting it, but I really couldn't finish the whole thing. I sort of just wanted to breathe!

The next day I felt kind of sick and sniffling, January weather I suppose. I tried to smoke a cigarette all day, but every time I'd get the smoke near me, I would sneeze to death nonstop until I put it out. I've smoked when I had bronchitis so bad I would have coughing fits that lasted ten minutes and left me purple and throwing up. Nothing stopped me from smoking when I wanted a cigarette! So I didn't successfully smoke that day, and on the next day, I started Diane's classes first thing in the morning. I couldn't wait to smoke, but I never did, for another month anyway.

I started smoking twice through the winter, a week each time. Once I'd start the weekend workshops, I could stop again easily. The breathing made me feel so much better, it was simple to quit. The last time I smoked was right before I came to summer camp. There was too much time before summer camp, after Adnan left. I had no workshops with sweet clean air to remind me of my newly found breath. So the smoky environment at my workplace won.

It's almost been two months now. In ordinary time, it's nothing, but I feel like I've breathed myself into a new life time, a new body and new head space. Space being the key word here! I really can't tolerate the frenzied energy of smokers. So I'll try to keep my peaceful state for awhile. The change in conditioning is too great for me to express right now, but a lot of the negative stuff about myself and flaws and faults and negative thoughts about myself were all very much a part of smoking. So when I am farther away from it all I will try to put it into words. Thank you, Adnan.

"The moment is the corridor that opens on eternity. When you are not in the moment, it is like being lost in a dark, damp basement without windows and full of smoke." – Adnan

"To control oneself is better than to rule over a nation." -- Abraham Adham (who left his throne to search for the truth)

Gwen Tastes the Spirit
Gwen Gosé

Just before I met Adnan, my boyfriend and I passed the time in the evenings in front of the TV stuffing down huge juicy steaks and baked potatoes accompanied by beer, a quart of Coke, chips and bags of our favorite cookies. Before we drifted into complete unconsciousness for the night, I would manage to smoke another pack of cigarettes to meet the quota of two packs a day, the other pack having been nervously puffed away while at work. In fact, since I was 13 years old and was first daring to carry cigarettes in my purse, I must have had a halo of smoke about my head – making the reading of my aura very cloudy! Because the quantity of cigarettes made my mouth dry and have a bad taste, I chewed gum all day and all night and drank coffee and liquor, which went so perfectly with the smoke flavor.

On weekends, we would go out for all-you-can-eat seafood dinners with friends. My favorite was to start with the cold-boiled shrimp with red sauce and a cigarette, and keep cigarettes going through the whole meal. You take a shrimp, then a puff and chew them both together for Marlboro-smoked shrimp, after which you wash each bite down with a "swig" of a salty-rimmed margarita. After the cold-boiled shrimp came the fried shrimp, and then the crabmeat dipped in butter sauce, then the fried crab, then the stuffed crab, then the broiled flounder, then the fried flounder and later the fried chicken.

It was my mother-in-law who introduced me both to cuisine and culinary delights and to consciousness work. She made the ritual morning coffee so perfectly in the electric brewer and always served it in beautiful china cups. On special occasions, we would take coffee after dinner and she would bring out the cherry liqueur to accompany the coffee. For a time, I submitted to her influence and tried to become a lady of etiquette and culture, but secretly I preferred my large glass of bourbon and Seven-Up to a cup of coffee chased with a petite parcel of sweet syrup. She also introduced me to rum cake (the one to which you start adding the rum six months before Christmas), brandy balls, beer burgers, cheese and wine fondue, cherries/brandy jubilee, and the secret starter recipe for a potent fruit compote that could be kept "alive" for years and passed down from generation to generation. On my own, I discovered the best use of my blender was for frozen strawberry daiquiris and the best way to drink beer was with raw oysters on the half shell, as looking for the pearl keeps you alert so you can drive home.

One time I almost became quite pure when my husband and I were living in British Honduras in the 60's. We were starting to run out of money and the canned goods we had brought with us had already dwindled, so we ate red beans and rice which we sometimes flavored with salt pork when our native helper brought it in from the nearby village (which happened to be called Boom Village) and with the beans and rice, sometimes we might have parrot or turtle stew. We stole fresh cucumbers from the field of a commercial grower and bought bananas and locally baked white bread and sweet cakes and drank Belizean Rum and cashew wine. My supply of American cigarettes had long ago been depleted so all that was available were filterless Mexican ovals or other types equally harsh and irritating to the throat. It was then that I had the novel inspiration to collect the used tobacco of the very tail-end of a finished cigarette, which after a period of aging and collecting I would then re-roll using the paper in which the homemade white bread was wrapped. So I was practically a vegetarian and had cut way down on the smoking! This technique of rolling the cigarettes worked fine until the store changed the type of paper they used to wrap the bread with, but by then we were about to return to the states anyway.

After having spent these several months of quasi-purity in the flat savannah meadows and palmettos of British Honduras, washing clothes by hand in rain water collected from the roofs of our tents, cooking over an outdoor wood fire and listening to Billy Graham on the BBC, I was ready for "something more" and longed for our return to the states. It was because of this state of openness and thirst for "something more" that, after our return, I found myself very attracted to a book my mother-in-law offered me called Consciousness. I poured over the words which came like a cool nectar from heaven to my dry parched heart. Later, I went with her to the weekly gatherings of a small group of spiritualists that she was involved with and tried to sift through the impressions I was getting from the experiences she would relate to me and from the readings of the mediums presiding at the gatherings who were able to see your spirit guides and other important dead people who apparently hover around the living ones in order to offer their assistance. At that time, I had enough trouble trying to relate to my own family, let alone trying to relate to a family of spirit guides floating around in my smoke, so my interest became diverted and grew and expanded to encompass plain old concepts like positive thinking, "I'm okay, you're okay," Remember, Be Here Now, the collective consciousness and the Fourth Way. All this heavy consciousness work required prolonged periods of relaxation and creative exploration which was accomplished by getting stoned and looking at M.C. Escher prints or Beardsley, or getting stoned and reading Richard Brautigan, or getting stoned and composing songs and painting trees of purple grapes or getting stoned and taking a candle lit bath with a friend that looked like Cat Stevens but couldn't sing like him.

Then one day I made a list of things that needed changing in my life. I only remember one word from that ancient list and it was "purity." Not long after the list, a friend of my boyfriend's invited me to a class of Adnan's in Houston. The class was held in the living room of a little white frame house. I can't recall much of what happened that evening, but I most probably must have been shocked to be sitting on the floor doing strange exercises in some stranger's house. The next thing I knew, Adnan had us standing up in two tight-knit circles, holding hands and swaying back and forth chanting *Allah hu*, while he circumnavigated the chanting circles and intensified the chant by beating on his drum. Time disappeared and the self disappeared and then either Kundalini was rising or I had an out of the body experience or I saw God, I'm not sure which, but the experience was manifested by a total loss of control – something like a holy rollers church meeting except that I wasn't speaking in tongues or rolling on the floor, but I was "puttin' up a holler". The rest of the evening was very grounding in comparison: Adnan served Baghdad ice cream and a man showed pictures of his wedding ceremony which had taken place during Adnan's previous summer camp.

Before dashing out of there for a cigarette, I must have connected with Manny, who was assisting Adnan with the music, only to discover that we worked on the same floor and in the same department in the mega-complex of the Texas Medical Center. Manny offered Sufi classes in Adnan's absence. So I went to Manny's classes for a few months until one day Manny suggested I go to a weekend workshop of Adnan's to be held in Philadelphia. I did.

This was the furthest distance north I had ever traveled outside of Texas. There were so many new experiences in just that one weekend, like sleeping on the floor and sleeping on the floor with a houseful of strangers, whirling for the first time in a huge gymnasium (I lasted about five minutes), seeing the spontaneous dance of a belly dancer who was moved by the music, and watching the concentration game: two people gaze at one another from across the room in a mystical concentration match.

Riding around in a car with Adnan was fun. He carried a tape player with him on his lap wherever he went. There was always so much activity and interesting things happening that I would almost forget to smoke. But one time I was trying to nonchalantly go out, during a break, for a cigarette and Adnan intercepted me in order to get a lesson on how to inhale properly. From then on I knew, the heat was on in relation to that habit. Later, Adnan was to define Sufism for us as meaning purity or submission and purity had been a word on my list of desired changes.

Another weekend followed in New York City. There was more whirling, this time outside in the grass at the St. John the Divine Cathedral, but also inside as I recall groups of three people whirled together surrounded by a larger group who were chanting and drumming and they would end by singing some kind of harmonics when all the voices would blend into a heavenly chorus of sound.

A few months later Adnan returned to Houston for another weekend. Before it started, Adnan said he could completely change me and I would become the center of the universe. Even with that stimulus, the workshop hit me pretty hard and, in fact, I was almost not able to do the work at all. I remember being very touched to hear Adnan play the finger cymbals and then to hear the Koran sung afterwards, but when he asked us to play a game and shout loud, louder, loudest the name of any person we loved, I had to leave the room crying and didn't come back until the next day.

Quite a few of the Houston people went to that next summer camp. I took a car load, which proved to be very stressful. Everybody wanted to take a turn driving, each with their own peculiarities, while the others were constantly giving each other foot massages. By the time we arrived at the camp in North Carolina, I had a throbbing toothache and couldn't even go into the workshop because the whole building seemed to be quaking from the vibration of a drumming tape being played on the maximum volume and my tooth was doing its own drumming. Nevertheless, changes started happening immediately. A medicine I had been taking continually for the past five years to control a nervous intestine disorder was stopped completely the first day of camp. The toothache resolved itself. My diet totally changed as habitual eating and drinking patterns were becoming affected. The old habits were being replaced by new ones, like eating dates stuffed with cream cheese and walnuts during the break time. The strangest experience came as a result of trying to fast. It had never occurred to me that any benefit could be received from not eating for a few days. I decided to do one day and that was the longest day of my life! Toward the end, I was literally watching the clock in anticipation of the 24th hour when I could eat again.

Adnan had mentioned that the Sufi work was a science, so I went into the nearest town with one of the Houston people for a little experimentation to see what breakfast would be like. I was shocked. Something had really changed within me that I couldn't see while absorbed in the workshop. There was almost nothing to order from the menu due to the reversal of preferences that had taken place. Whereas previously one of my favorite things was a restaurant breakfast of scrambled eggs, bacon and sausage with frequent refills on coffee dowsed with milk and sugar and cigarettes before, during and after, now all there was to do was stare at my watery scrambled eggs and bother the waitress about the absence of whole wheat bread and honey.

Before the Sufi work and following my divorce, I had been in psychotherapy for two years during which time I had been encouraged to keep the typical journal, so there was a volume of fragmented and disjointed thought patterns and songs of lost love and disillusionment all preserved in writing. That first summer with Adnan began to tap a more connected center within me and recharge my dying spirit which resulted in the following writings which I believe depict an awakening and an opening to a new life:

Ego Image
Fragile as a lacy leaf, the ego sees itself in disbelief.
Thinking itself a rock among pebbles,
It dreams it's a freeway
Though just a creek bed narrow.

Soul Foot
Straw feet — the pasture releases its foliage
to my each step.
Fern-filled forest floor — so gentle to my feet,
cushions of my soul.

New Me
> I am in every movement, a dance. I am in every
> spoken word, a song. I am in every thought, a
> moment, non-reflective of one past or to come.

Crimson Cloud
> Expand.
> It is limitless beyond these filmy edges.
> My God, my ears are bounding with these notes.
> My eyes are swelling amid the beauty.
> Explore.
> My head swells in the luxury of being present.
> My nostrils are intoxicated by these vapors:
> Perfumed shadows reflect the brilliance of the now.
> Token glimpses. Crimson cloud.

I remember new sensations and experiences like going out to sit in the woods on a favorite rock and just being there. And while passing the trees, I remember feeling very connected to them and could see them in a new way. These experiences astounded me as I considered myself very polluted physically and immature spiritually. Yet the work was powerful enough to convert all that negative energy, conditioning and pollution of spirit, at least temporarily, into something positive, beautiful, contented, peaceful and connected.

At the end of the six weeks, I felt a major shift had happened in terms of redirecting my energy toward working on myself (under the guidance of Adnan) and away from the unfulfilling struggle to seek romantic love. Just as I was preparing to leave the camp and thinking that I had completed the process, it was over, and I would never see these people again; it occurred to me to say goodbye to Adnan, as there was a rumor that he might return to Baghdad. When the shock of potentially losing Adnan finally reached its mark, I was magically transformed. My senses were flooded by the realization that rather than being completed, the process had just begun, which served to rinse even more of my tobacco-stained spirit clean.

The ride back to Houston was remarkable. My companion and I were determined to stay on the right program as we had been advised that the first week after camp was crucial. Almost immediately, I experienced a remarkable lessening of fear and other negativity which became apparent while doing some swimming and diving at a campsite along the way. I was doing dives that exceeded anything I had ever been able to do following rigorous and repetitive practice during hot Texas summers. Now I could spring up on the board and sail into the sky without fear and with pleasure.

After about six weeks back into the routine of life, I noticed that the effects of the six weeks at summer camp were starting to fade. Adnan had said you get what you earn. Six weeks doing the work had earned six weeks of protected positive energy. Among the most delightful examples of this new energy was waking up in the morning and hearing an involuntary praise to God rush out on the first breath. Quite a change from reaching for a cigarette first thing in the morning. At one point, I tried to put that new energy to a test by going out with friends for a birthday celebration and allowing myself to drink alcohol one last time. I kept drinking and drinking until I had consumed four tequila sunrise drinks and nothing had happened. I was so shocked by that experience that I never touched anything alcoholic again. The desire for it had absolutely gone. The thought to even do it must have been the shadow of its existence in exit.

Cigarettes presented more of a difficulty; they were somehow more firmly rooted and interlaced in my negative conditioning. So even after I thought I was rid of the habit, I found it still had a potential power to strike out like a scorpion's tail and attract me back with its poison.

Being faced with the struggle with the negative self was so completely consuming that I never really had the strength to apply my own will to it (it being a rather weak entity anyway). Instead, I gradually learned to trust in the Sufi work, and in myself and what we were doing, and let the process take care of itself. I learned that it was better to let go and not stand in the way of destiny and not try to manipulate the creation with a negative-based ego; better to let the Creator do the creation and for me to try to stay connected to the presence. Around Thanksgiving time, I started feeling my positive energy fading even more, so I wanted to do another workshop with Adnan when he called to let me know about the Thanksgiving workshop in Chicago . . . (to be continued).

And God said, "Believers, be patient and strive against your natural desires and maintain this striving manfully."

Perception
James Dillehay, 1984

One day we were sent outside to chant *Allah Akbar*, inwardly awhile, then outwardly and then just sitting and watching the nature around us. Three times I went through this cycle, each turn producing a new level of sight and feeling. The last was the most powerful, as I opened my eyes to a vibrant, radiant world. The trees and the earth and the space in between shimmered with color, all doing nature's belly dance. I had walked up the mountain a way to do this chanting and I felt now, as I started down, a perfect peace and harmony with all the trees and the earth and the birds and the air and the wind. I came back reluctantly, feeling that the business of camp would bring me down.

Quite by accident on my walk, I had discovered a hidden waterfall that made beautiful music as the falling water burst against a pool, preciously surrounded and protected by its walls, a secret treasure of water and sound. Suspiciously, the music was very like the background of Adnan's songs. I seemed to be held still by the vibrations and so I sat rather high up and watched the sky and mountains. How unusual for me to have words to describe what I see: Against a powdery blue sky, the ash grey and marshmallow clouds slowly drift over the mountains and cast their shadows in patterns never repeated, ever again. Trees green of jade and watermelon rind, the ruddy camel browns of the earth, ancient grey tree trunks, great old monuments sculpted by time. Stones like steps of pearl, leading nowhere, leading everywhere. My eye sees within a circle. The sky is a circle. The earth is a circle. The water falls in circles and circles. Each note of the music is a circle, breaking the next circle of the next note and then the next, and the next. And who knows what the next circle will be?

"Make your thought like tender harp music that brings pleasure to the one who hears it, and the heart will dance on its tune." — Adnan

Diane Gives Up a Life of Cocaine to Breathe Spirit
Diane Reichard

The day that Adnan's Sufi work entered my life was the day my life completely turned around and transformed. When I met Adnan five years ago my life was totally black. I was as low as I could be and I was totally out of touch with myself and the world around me. I was a cocaine addict and dealer, taking cocaine from morning until night every day. I was like walking death with dark circles around my eyes. I weighed about ninety pounds and I did not care when or if I ate food. I would force myself to have tea and toast in the evening just to put something in my stomach. I did not work a job. I paid some of my bills with the money from the cocaine I sold, but mostly I left the bills unpaid and put the cocaine in my body. I could not sleep much because the cocaine keeps you awake and jittery. I had no pastimes other than sitting all night with my friends, doing the cocaine until my lips would turn blue and the sun would be rising. I might as well have been dead and I almost did die when I started using a needle to put the cocaine in my arm to get more of it. I came very close to an overdose.

It was only about three or four months later that a friend talked me into taking a belly dance class with her. I did not want to do it, but this friend really pushed me and my boyfriend wanted me out of his way for a while so I agreed to do it. It turned out that the class was taught by a student of Adnan's, Janet Periolat, and I really liked the class, although I found it hard to breathe properly, since I was doing the cocaine. I liked the class enough that I wanted to do more and Janet told me that her teacher, Adnan, was coming in a few weeks and that I would like his classes even better.

Now I had never done any spiritual work in my life, nor meditation, although I knew these things existed from reading a little bit about them. But I really had no idea what I was getting into. I did a few evening sessions with Adnan and I loved them. Then I did a weekend workshop. This was the most powerful experience in my life, and I will never forget it. It was the turning point for me. I think that weekend Adnan saved my life.

It was not gradual for me. The power of the Sufi work took over me that weekend and I had no control over what happened. I chanted, exercised and danced with the group, but it was like my mind was suspended. It was so deep for me that time stood still and I could not think for the two days of the workshop.

Much of the time I felt I was dreaming. It felt strange but wonderful. I was a wooden puppet on a string and Adnan was the puppeteer pulling all the strings and rearranging everything inside of me, making me come back to life.

Sunday night I was in a new state. Adnan told me to go look at my eyes in the mirror. I had never seen them like this before, so wide open and filled with energy. It was incredible! Adnan told me he had connected my eyes with my soul. I had never felt so elated and so full inside, as if my body would burst. It was as if I had been numb all over and now for the first time I could feel myself alive. I was in awe of Adnan and his Sufi work.

I went home that night and as I walked in the door, my boyfriend, who was across the room, looked up, saw my face and was shocked. He said very seriously, "You are different!" That night he kept asking me to do some cocaine with him and I finally agreed. I could not believe how bad it made me feel and how much it ruined my good feeling from the Sufi work. I got angry and decided right then I would never take cocaine again and I never did touch it again.

All of this happened to me from only one weekend of Sufi work! Since then I have continued to do the Sufi these last five years. I am still not as strong as I would like to be. There are times when I leave the work to do other things which I think are "very important," only to find out each time that I am wrong. Every time I come back to the work, Adnan patiently shows me the way to get back on the right track. It seems like he never tires or runs out of energy to help me and hundreds of his other students. It really amazes me!

Now I am to the point where I know that the Sufi work is the most important thing in my life. I look at all the ways I have changed and grown and I cannot believe it! The drugs are gone, my diet has completely changed, no more Coca-Cola and junk food, and my face is no longer yellow and tense, but is rosy and shining. My body has changed and I can move in ways I have never moved before. The tension in my stomach is going away. I am able to work good jobs now like bookkeeping and accounting and I am able to relax and enjoy people again without so much emotional tension and paranoia. I feel like a worthwhile human being and I can see the beauty in the world and breathe it in the air. I can feel the love of God around me that I have never felt before, even throughout my Catholic upbringing. I can dance and feel the energy flowing. I can laugh and I can pray now, using the powerful chapters of the Koran in my daily life and seeing the power and the positive effect they have. I never experienced any of these things before doing the Sufi work.

I feel stronger yet softer, more independent, more compassionate, much more aware and, most of all, much more at peace inside myself and with the world. I take life slower now, watching more and savoring more and being part of it instead of avoiding it. There is so much to see and do and every little thing can be a joy.

All of these things are the result of only one experience in my life: the Sufi work that Adnan teaches. None of the books I had read, nor the many counselors and psychologists I had paid, nor the drugs I took, nor the boyfriends I lived with ever made even a slight difference in my life except to confuse and weaken me. It was only the Sufi work that had the impact on my life to completely change me inside and out toward the positive.

I have no way to thank Allah for dropping in my lap this wonderful gift of the Sufi work just when I needed it, nor can I begin to thank Adnan for always guiding me through it.

"If you are grateful I will add more favors unto you." – Koran

Stacy Conquering the Asthma
Stacy Kaser

Yesterday, chanting *Ya hadi* among the tall Ponderosa pines of the national forest, I suddenly realized that I was doing exactly what I should be doing and where I should be doing it. This, after years of searching and wondering if I'd ever find "my path." This work here at camp is my path, at least for this moment in time.

The summer did not start with these feelings. The first two weeks or so were very difficult, and I'm sure that there will be difficult times ahead. Facing one's fears, attachments, anger and ego issues is seldom loads of fun and is rarely completely finished. I began to question the wisdom of coming here. "This is my vacation?" I asked.

Because of my great capacity for self-criticism, I perceived everyone at camp assessing and judging my progress in the work. Because of my capacity to pull in and put walls up, I perceived people at camp ignoring and isolating me. (I realize that this doesn't logically fit with the previous supposition, but, hey, it's my negative self talking, what can I say?) Because of my capacity to analyze and re-analyze and over-analyze, I had worked out a formula where by Adnan could not do anything which I could interpret as positive feedback: if he frowned, it meant that I was tense or negative or stupid; if he smiled at me, it meant that I was really stupid and needed coddling to stay in the work; if he interacted with me in a playful way, it meant that he thought I was childish and spiritually immature. The list could go on. The quantity and variety of crap my negative self, my mind, can generate is truly astounding.

Last year, when I came here for my two week vacation, I felt a connection only to the dancing. I believed, naively, that I could choose to do only this portion of the work. I resented Adnan terribly for the very uncomfortable state I experienced. But, after the two weeks, I began to feel positive effects — especially from the chanting which I continued to do at home and at work. As a result of the two weeks plus the winter workshops Diane held and contact with the camp-sufis, I was able to make some big changes in my diet. In one year (or less), I gave up sugar, almost all dairy, my last bit of caffeine-tea, and I'm working now on wheat. Because of these delayed reactions I experienced last year, I really don't know what changes my time here this year will bring.

This brings me to the issue of health. I have what is medically termed "severe, chronic, bronchial asthma." I've had it since I was three months old. I've been on daily medication since that time and hospitalized frequently when it has become more seriously acute. One notable hospital occasion, on Halloween of 1982, (during which I almost became a real ghost), I fought strenuously for 36 to 48 hours to live. Although I never want to repeat this, it is the most valuable memory I have. Few people get that close to death and make it back (so the Emergency Room and Intensive Care Unit doctors say). It instantly prioritizes your life. That's the point when my search for better health and spirit really began — indirectly at first, directly for the past 4-5 years.

Recently, in the fall of 1989, I started acupuncture treatments for my asthma, just before I began taking Sufi workshops with Diane. For the past year and a half, I haven't seen the inside of a hospital, I've avoided the intense medications I've needed occasionally in the past and I've begun to reduce my daily medications. In general, I feel much stronger and healthier, but I have a ways to go. I see that this work has improved my health and I'm open to further improvement. It would literally be a dream coming true, but I feel I must be somewhat cautious in my optimism, and stay in this moment and this breath, and in this moment, I love the chanting, I love the whirling, and I love the state I get to in the workshops.

"Seek excellence and you will be excellent. Seek less than excellence and you will be less than excellent." – Adnan

"The ego is a dark, fanatic force, the word compromise is alien to it." – Adnan

A Letter to Lamia in Baghdad
(by Janet Norquist, October, 1983)

Dear Lamia,

It was a thrill to be able to speak with you all the way from Baghdad! It was only a few words while you waited for Adnan to come to the telephone, but, nevertheless, I am inspired to write a letter to you. Adnan tells us that you're a teacher of English, so I am confident that you will understand what I write. It must be nice living in Baghdad where so many of the tales of the "Arabian Nights" took place. Adnan has told us some similar stories from his own experience.

It is true what I told you on the telephone, that Adnan is an extraordinarily good man. There are thousands of his students, like me, who will say the same thing. Adnan has shown us a life of Reality (and the way of Allah) virtually unknown in the western world. Through his teaching of the Sufi way, he has brought countless people from lives of misery to lives which are beautiful and deep. He has helped to change even the worst cases, like criminals or drug addicts. I myself was one of those who took drugs and drank alcohol. I lived in New York City, and, although I led a very successful life financially, with a prestigious career at the "New York Times" newspaper and with many "successes" as a singer, I was still very unhappy. I did not know my "truthful self," *al nafs al mu'tamana.*

I turned to every other kind of comfort, including drugs and alcohol. After I met Adnan and began doing the Sufi work, I quickly and immediately stopped all of those bad habits. I never touched liquor, drugs or even cigarettes any more. The same thing has happened to many of Adnan's students after studying with him. Adnan has shown us the way to a much deeper satisfaction.

As I said, just before I met Adnan, I was looking for ways to understand life. I was very confused. No one would ever think so to look at me, however, because most people in America are constantly in a confused state. It takes a spiritual longing and some kind of spiritual work, such as Adnan offers, to break out of the confusion. You can imagine, the typical life of an American is to watch television and eat junk food, to go to a job, and then repeat the process every day. Most people eat enormous amounts of sugar, coffee, pork, all kinds of unhealthy foods, and they drink alcoholic beverages daily. And without the slightest idea of what spirituality or the reality is.

For one year before I met Adnan I went to a psychologist named Janet Pfunder. I poured out my distress to her and, because I mentioned my longing for "reality", she suggested I try something deeper. It was my greatest luck and good fortune that Janet happened to be a student of Adnan Sarhan.

One weekend she invited me to come to do the Sufi work because Adnan happened to be in New York giving a workshop. It was exactly what I was searching for. I couldn't understand it intellectually, but something told me I didn't need to understand it in that way. Furthermore, I no longer felt the need for psychology. I continued with the Sufi work, and now I can hardly believe the changes in myself. All of the worry, sorrow, tension and pain have simply evaporated, and my life has become beautiful, calm and relaxed.

Adnan has taught thousands of us the deep power of the Holy Quran that opens doors to inner knowledge, a power and knowledge we would otherwise never have known. I now know twelve suras in Arabic, and I do the "salat" prayer five times daily. Adnan has also taught us to chant the beautiful names of God in Arabic. We also do the Ramadan fast every year at the prescribed time, and we continue to do the Ramadan fast during the rest of the year, too, any time we are doing the Sufi work with Adnan. For this, I thank God and I am deeply grateful to your brother, Adnan, as are all of his students.

I would like to tell you about my parents. When I first wrote home to them about Adnan and the Sufi work, they became very suspicious. In fact, they were "beside themselves" with anxiety and fear. They were certain that I had joined a weird religious mind-control cult led by a strange "guru." They were frantic with fear. I went home to Wisconsin to visit them, to reassure them that I was not forced into anything and that I was still their loving daughter. It was not easy, since my father is a Christian, Presbyterian minister who had a blind hatred for Arabs and anything vaguely related to Islam. But with the patience Adnan taught me, I was able to show them that I was fine. They calmed down for a while. Meanwhile, my youngest sister, Lois, noticed the profound change in me. She told me that I had a calmness and a compassion about me. I never encouraged her to try the Sufi work herself because I didn't want to upset my parents, but, of her own accord, she simply announced that she was coming and asked me to pick her up at the airport.

Lois was epileptic, taking a very heavy medication, Phenobarbital, prescribed to her by doctors. The month before she came to do the Sufi work, she had five epileptic seizures (even while taking the Phenobarbital). After she came here to do the Sufi work, she had one more seizure during the first month, and now, one and a half years later she still hasn't had any more seizures. She is completely in control of her epilepsy. The doctors can't believe it. You may know that some causes for epilepsy are tension, poor diet and a deep disturbance in the brain. Adnan's techniques with the drumming and fasting and other Sufi exercises go directly to the problem, and are able to control the seizures. (Incidentally, there are two other people here who used to have epileptic seizures, but now are changed because of Adnan's work.)

Last spring, my parents were still suspicious, even though they could see that we had changed in such a positive way. We invited them to come to New Mexico to see for themselves. When they arrived, I could see that my father already had preconceptions. He was very angry and confused. After one day he and my mother left in a rage. But then Adnan invited him to return to talk to the people about Jesus and Christianity. My father agreed to come back. He had a long talk with Adnan after which he had completely changed his attitude. Seeing that Adnan was in no way threatening to him, he began to open his mind. The next two weeks of my parents' visit was very pleasant, and they left happily, and with the intention of visiting again. My father also invited Adnan to come to his church to teach Sufi to his congregation. It seems that everyone who comes in contact with Adnan is affected in a positive way. Adnan is truly a man of God.

Music has always been important to me. I studied it all of my life. I started with piano lessons when I was five years old and eventually, when I went to college I began training as an opera singer. In New York I sang for the Bel Canto Opera Company, and with the New York Philharmonic Orchestra in ensembles. I was invited to sing as a soloist with the Stuttgart Chamber Orchestra in Germany, and at the Beaubourg Center in Paris, France. But it was not satisfying to me. I quit singing completely...that is, until Adnan came into my life. Before I met him, I was never acquainted with Arabic music. Soon I realized that Arabic music has a deep inner power which is missing in most Western music. When Adnan introduced me to the profoundly beautiful music of Om

Kalthoum, Farid, Fayrouz and others, it opened up a new world for my true voice, not the one which I "learned" in school in the artificial way. I began singing along with the Arabic music and have already learned hundreds of melodies, and the Arabic words for a least twenty songs. The Arabic music has awakened something deep in my soul.

Adnan says that some day you might come to the United States to visit. I hope so. I would like very much to meet you. I would love to visit Iraq, but at this time no American citizens are allowed unless they are Iraqi born. Some day it will be possible. I am sure you will be very happy to see Adnan again after so many years.

Sincerely yours with kindest regards, Janet Norquist

From Paralysis to Paradise
Susan Whitefeather-Meadow, 1993

I first attended one of Adnan's workshops approximately fifteen years ago, and I experienced the healing power of his drumming. That day, I felt something leave me, something like a dark veil that I had been holding onto with great tenacity, but little awareness. I sought to do the work again, but somehow the time must not have been right. I could never find anyone who knew when Adnan would be in the area; and the few times I heard he was here, he had already left. Several weeks ago, a friend told me that Adnan was going to be in Denver and Boulder, and gave me the number to call for information.

The first workshop I attended was in the evening. During the floor exercise work, I became somewhat excruciatingly aware of what seemed to be energy blockages at various points throughout my body. These were not the same thing as muscle cramps, stiffness or soreness (although those were there, too). The best analogy I can draw would be an electrical short circuit, a place where electrical energy is blocked in its flow, and the resulting heat often can burn up the circuit. If I substitute pain for heat, that's kind of how it seemed. Then I attended the weekend workshop. I hoped the perception I had of energy being blocked would be helped. It was. I was not, however, prepared for the extent of the physical changes that occurred.

To give a little history, I am forty-four years old. When I was eighteen, I was in an accident that severed the tendons and muscle on the inside of the calf of my right leg. The surgeons believed it unlikely that I would walk again, but they spliced the tendons and repaired the muscle anyway. I did regain the full use of my leg, but the right leg below the knee was about one-half inch sorter than my left leg. I began to experience tingling in my thigh. It spread and soon the outer third of my thigh, from the top of my knee to the top of my leg, was numb to sensation, and when I stood for more than a few minutes, the pain and burning were intense. I was told by my physician that the problem was due to pinching of a larger nerve going through my pelvis, because I was <u>permanently</u> misaligned due to the differential in the length of my two legs. He said that it would get worse over time and that the nerve would become permanently damaged.

The pain had become markedly worse. It was like an ever-present companion who sometimes nagged and sometimes shrieked. About six months ago, I consulted with two M.D.'s who were orthopedic specialists. Both rendered the same diagnosis and prognosis. "The nerve is permanently damaged. You can expect it to become even worse. Learn to live with it. Practice pain management," they both said. I had been doing those things for many years. I had taken a philosophical approach, seeing the pain as a way to cultivate endurance and courage. It was my way of reconciling myself to the inevitable, as I had accepted the situation as irreversible.

Saturday evening I went home from the workshop. I noticed the oddest sensation. I had feeling in my right thigh! The numb spot had shrunk to an area about the size of the palm of my hand. When I awoke on Sunday, the numb spot was gone. I have not experienced the pain since that time. The muscle tone is virtually identical in both thighs and this has not been true for years. Thank you again, Adnan.

Sian Frees Herself from the Fog of London Under the New Mexico Sun
Sian Davey

In my working life, as for most people, I was required to be "in my head" and "in charge." I worked for a large corporation in England, first as a manager then a trainer/consultant, for ten years. We were a communications company — and that was basically my job, to help it communicate with itself. I became an interpreter, spending much time entering into other people's worlds to listen and observe, in order to be able to describe them to other people. But I became increasingly aware that I had lost my sense of my world and of my self.

Time became impossible after awhile, trying to juggle my old friends and interests, a 60 hour week, and new pursuits. I spent a lot of time in my car thinking about where I had been and worrying about how late I would be for my next meeting, and making appointments for more meetings. I was so much in the future, that whenever I came down to earth I had to keep going back to the past to keep myself up to date with what had been happening. I seemed to be in a constant state of fighting — fighting fatigue, fighting at work, fighting the schedules, fighting guilt, fighting the traffic — and all through sheer willpower!

Four years ago I had begun to search through various ingredients: massage, meditation, movement and dance, some psychotherapy, much reading. And I began to meet many people involved in similar quests. Coming here to the Sufi work, I have a sense of coming home. There is a strong sense of community and sharing here, like a big family — something I have always wanted to be part of. I can just enjoy being myself and being enough. I see myself reflected in so many mirrors around me. Some qualities I like, many I want to change, and some new ones I want to learn from others. I am learning tolerance and patience as much with myself as with others.

For myself — I still love the dancing, although blind-folded I like the best. I think I have finally got the hang of whirling with a little help from my friends, despite having fallen at the first few attempts! But my favorite, I think, is the chanting. I love chanting by myself, especially in the woods. I can really connect it with my love of nature. I am sure the trees and rocks enjoy it, and that the clouds dance with me sometimes. And I love chanting with the group, too. It is such a powerful way to share God, and to share ourselves, to participate in our miraculous universe! The slow movements and the breathing exercises give me such peace.

Peace. Before the Sufi work I used to meditate often, and be in the elements to pray. Especially the sea — it gives me such a sense of timelessness and proportion. But my feeling is that this place is something different, or somewhere of a different order. A place of silence, of peace, and home.

"Respect the time and the time will respect you. And the time will be your guide to the hidden space where the hidden reality manifests itself to you." — Adnan

Leslie Discovers the Secret to Life
Leslie Williams

October, 1994: I had a dream shortly after the last Christmas workshop. In the dream, Adnan said to a friend of mine, "Leslie can no longer walk on two paths, she must choose." This dream affected me greatly because I had also been feeling that even though I had made major changes in my life since the 3-1/2 years I've been doing the work, I still did indeed walk on two paths. I was still not willing to give up certain attitudes and ways of living, of certain lifestyles that were contradictory to the work. And then I had this dream. And it became so clear to me that to do the Sufi work meant living purely in everything that I do, in all my relationships, in my work life, in what I ate, in what I thought, in all of my actions; that I couldn't do the work and then go out to a nightclub and drink beer or allow the struggles of life to completely rule my emotions; and that to do the work meant a commitment, a development of concentration and most of all a surrender and trust to the experience of practicing Sufism.

I feel from this summer a tremendous rising up of my own power and strength; I feel more me, without my usual cosmetics. I've often considered myself a strong person, capable of getting what I need and want, however, this new power and strength is of a different kind. This is built almost out of a feeling in myself of unraveling, like being peeled off and the "who I really am" is what came out. The new who I am isn't based on manipulation, or my charms, or any of the abundant ego skills I'm so good at, but rather this strength feels as if it is built out of the intelligence of my intuition.

Fasting during my last month at camp had a profound effect on me. This, I believe, was critical in pushing me further into the work. With fasting, it took away more resistance and all I wanted to do was chant, be in nature, draw, and be mesmerized by the poignant beauty of the world in each moment. And then the experience after the fast got even stronger. I realized that I no longer had any longing for anything, that I had actually found the "It" that I had always been looking for, with a complete and total fulfillment and contentment. I felt like I discovered the secret to life!

It's only been three weeks since leaving camp, but I notice a few things: I have no desire to overeat and I have no food cravings. I'm satisfied with small amounts of food and all I want is simple food. Usually after camp, I spend the first two weeks fulfilling all the food fantasies I had during the workshop, but this time I feel detached from food. This is a big change.

I feel that what Sufi does is give us skills, practices - almost like a code of behavior - that we can use to bring understanding to life and to give us a way to deal with the challenges of every day life. My goal is to bring these skills into everything that I do. It will take a lot of discipline, of checking myself constantly, or re-remembering what is important and of developing concentration of the mind and thought: the key to everything.

August, 1997: I feel like a sensitive new flower. I feel my heart. I feel the abundance of all there is. I feel the incredible gratitude of what you have brought to my life. I have never before appreciated to this extent the state of grace that comes over us in the work. For me, it is the quiet, the extraordinary perfume of peace and love that lays over like a warm blanket, soothing my mind and bringing me into God's light.

The work also gives me such an incredible feeling of freedom. It opens up infinite doors and infinite ways of living. It removes the walls and assumptions I hold onto and gives me new eyes to see with. It expands my world because possibilities become - oh, so possible.

A good example of such an opening of possibilities is my story of how I came to start my own successful import business. In 1990 when I first became involved in the Sufi work, something opened in me. The work made me expansive and gave me a sense of freedom and a feeling that I had the ability to do whatever I wanted to do. I noticed that self-created boundaries of what is or is not possible disappeared and I had a feeling of boundaryless freedom of living. Opportunities opened to me, as well.

I had always wanted to travel and go on an extended trip, such as to Morocco or Indonesia, just to have fun, enjoy myself and do something different. So after my first summer camp, I made a trip to Indonesia for 7 months. When I got back, I needed to get a job. Then I remembered the children's clothes that I had seen and loved in Indonesia and it just popped into my head to go back to Indonesia, buy some things and start my own import business. So within a month, I found a cheap airline ticket back to Indonesia through a courier company, went on a buying spree and came back to New York to sell things at street fairs. In two weekends, I had made back all my money!

I literally had to teach myself every aspect of running business from buying to customs rules and regulations, shipping and sales. Later, I decided to show the clothes at various international buyers' exhibitions, in addition to selling them at the street fairs. Because of the highly competitive market, I realized I had to have something different. Even though I had no design experience, I went back to Bali and started developing my own designs and fabric prints for children's clothes and had them manufactured in Bali for me. Since then, I've been successful in continuing to develop my business. Caring about what you do and loving it is the key to successful business. Like Adnan says, "When you have good intention, something good comes from it."

I've been doing the work now for seven years and for seven years, I've heard Adnan talk about not giving the negative self any attention and to kill any thought in the head that is negative and that negative thought brings negative action and positive thought brings positive action. Never before have I understood the power of this as I have this last year and throughout this summer. I now practice this as much as I can. I watch like a hawk my thinking, and if one negative thought comes, I try to recognize it and to cut it. I feel such gratefulness to know this and to experience it.

When I met you, I was like a starving, thirsty animal. I didn't even know there was food or drink in the world, only an unremitting yearning. Through the Sufi work, I've been fed and my thirst has been quenched. Adnan, thank you from the bottom of my heart for your guidance to spirit.

"A thought that originates in the spirit knows nothing but joy, tranquility and pleasure." – Adnan

"Good works are the result of good states. Good states rise from the stations wherein abide those who have spiritual realization." -- Ibn 'Ata'illah

The Sufi Experience
--A student's experience in Adnan's workshop

The Sufi experience is different for each individual depending on his capacities and his stage of evolution at any particular time. For me, right now, Sufi is a calming, a stilling, an openness to experience the now. It is a balance that creates stillness in motion and motion in stillness.

For me, Sufi is the path and the search for God as Unity, Harmony, and Truth. Sometimes the feeling is one of vibrating wordless ecstasy; often it is that of struggle and discipline.

But above and beyond all, Sufi is love.